MW01514518

GOD DIDN'T SAY THAT!

What You *Really* Need to Know to Live a Life of Radical Faith and Real Power

by

Mikaela Cade

Xulon
PRESS

God Didn't Say That!
by Mikaela Cade

Printed in the United States of America

ISBN 978-1-60791-824-0

Unless otherwise indicated, Scripture quotations are taken from the King James Version of the Bible.

www.xulonpress.com

To My Heavenly Father
Thank You for the privilege of sharing Your Word.
Your love and faithfulness to me have inspired
every part of this book.

*"For all things come of thee, and of thine own have we
given thee" (1 Chronicles 29:14)*

To My Husband
The longest pregnancy ever! Thank you for walking with
me every day and for your encouragement when I was too
tired to push.

To My Children
Thanks for your love, support, and challenge.
You make me live it better every day.

To My Mom
Thanks for everything you have given me. You gave me
life, you gave me a name, you named my first baby, and of
course my first book.

To VFGPS (past and present members)
Thanks for allowing me to serve you. You have enriched
my life and helped me more than you will ever know.

I love you all.

Table of Contents

Introduction

One morning as I was reading through the Gospel of Matthew, something hit me like a ton of bricks. Jesus said, "Ye have heard that it hath been said by them of old time, but I say unto you...." He kept saying it. Each time He made that statement He would expand on a common teaching and infuse it with truth and clarity. He provoked the people to think beyond what they had always understood or thought to be right. He challenged them to explore the deeper meaning of a life that honors God. He inspired them to radically change the quality and condition of their lives. In what could be considered "extreme" teaching, Jesus turned society upside down. He pushed the proverbial envelope. He gave religious pomposity its walking papers. His actions caused people to leave the confines of dead religious tradition and embrace the life God ordained. Jesus was and continues to be the quintessential kingdom teacher and preacher. After all, He is God.

The words He spoke revealed truth and power. Understanding great spiritual truth produces dramatic change. If the people received the truth, their lives would be transformed. What an incredible insight! Practical comprehension of the life-giving principle contained in the Word is the key to consistent and powerful kingdom living. The body of Christ can no longer simply understand the words of the law while lacking the experience of life the words bring us. We must embrace powerful living. It is God's plan that we experience a life of faith, power, and abundance given through His Word.

What I have found to be consistently true is that many people struggle with the practical application of God's Word. This struggle results in a life lived below the level ordained for them. The spiritual repercussions of a depressed life are evidenced in a lack of power, authority, and experience. Living below the position God established allows the struggle between the spirit and the flesh to continue. It causes a believer to lose hope. It can cause doubts about the truth and power of God's Word. It is problematic for true spiritual growth. God created you to live a life of radical faith. He created you to experience and demonstrate real power. He created you to have life, and life more abundantly. You can experience this by having a clearer understanding of what God really meant when He taught the people.

Everyday people deal with the issues of life the best way they can. They often struggle to make real, practical connections between their faith and their daily actions. They live each day obeying the Word as they understand it but fail to see the result that is often talked about, preached about, and expected. This can be very disheartening. Truth be told, many who serve the Lord may not experience the result they long for; the results their faith says is available to them. Does this mean God is wrong or has limited power? Absolutely not. It simply reveals a gap between where we are and where God wants us to be. We must close the gap. It is time to experience the life talked about in the Bible. It is time to close the gap between faith and experience. It is time for the kingdom of God to be manifested in earth through a prolific demonstration of powerful Christian living. I wrote *God Didn't Say That!* to help you accomplish just that—live the Christian life victoriously with knowledge, wisdom, and understanding.

A powerful Christian life is not measured by how big a church is or which church you attend. It doesn't have anything to do with a title given to you by man. A powerful Christian life is one that is full and complete, with respect to daily fellowship with God and walking in obedience to His Word. When you are living a powerful Christian life, every morning finds you excited and ready to reflect the glory of God. When you are living a powerful Christian life, you realize that you are like a prism, designed to reflect the glory and power of God back toward Him and also to send the rays of that life into the lives of those you encounter. This is life victorious, and it isn't reserved for a selected few. It is for you. It is for you now; you can stake your claim.

God Didn't Say That! will help clarify some of the commonly misunderstood principles of the Christian faith, the kinds of things commonly thought to be understood because they seem so simple. It contains twelve pillars for successful Christian living. The purpose is to move you toward a more fulfilling and exciting life of faith. *God Didn't Say That!* breaks up the fallow ground of intellectual Christianity to produce a harvest of true experiences with God. Every believer must know the Lord in a more intimate way. The shift from intellectual to experiential Christianity can be revolutionary for your life.

What is intellectual Christianity? I can probably explain it best through an example. Let's say you like a certain actor. You know all their movies and even some of their life story. Over the years you have found out little tidbits of information here and there, and you really feel as if you know them. One day you are sitting in a coffee shop and they walk in. You rush over and begin a conversation, feeling very familiar with them, but their response is not as warm as you would like. In fact, to you they seem cold and distant. You leave the coffee shop disheartened, and your opinion of them changes because they aren't all that you thought they were. You might even leave the coffee shop determined not to have anything else to do with them. The truth is you never really *knew* them, you only *knew about* them.

Knowing about someone doesn't constitute a relationship. If this is true for human relationships then it is true for the greatest relationship of our lives. Knowing about God and knowing Him are two completely different things, and the experience that comes from each is dramatically different. Think about your favorite actor again. If you continued to pursue them, security or the police may stop you because you might be considered a stalker conversely, if you continue to pursue God without respect of a relationship you would take on the same status- spiritual stalker. A spiritual stalker is a person who knows about God but is void of a true relationship with him. They live in a fantasy world never building a walk of faith but developing it out of their imagination. Intellectual Christianity is similar in that you might know about God, but the true intimacy found in relationship is absent from your encounters. *God Didn't Say That!* uncovers some of the keys to developing a more intimate relationship with God. There are three main points to each chapter: the problem, the truth, and its application in your life. Each chapter also addresses common thoughts or attitudes, reveals the myths associated with those thoughts, and then imparts truth according to the Word of God. Each chapter concludes with a prayer and space for your personal interaction with the material presented.

I pray that the words of this book will challenge you to rethink some of the patterns and habits you may have and exchange them for a fresh and more powerful perspective. The apostle Paul calls us to renew our minds and be transformed. A true understanding of the life-giving aspect of the Word will transform your life. It's time to break out of old patterns that do not serve you or glorify God and move into a place where you are able to prove the good, perfect, and acceptable will of God. Romans 12:2 says, "Be not conformed to this world but be ye transformed by the renewing of your mind that ye may prove what is that good and acceptable and perfect will of God." Your ability to prove or demonstrate the good, acceptable, and perfect will of God is found in understanding what God *did* say.

Let's begin our journey...

Chapter One

God Didn't Say...Apologize

_~_

_"If we confess our sins, He is faithful and righteous
to forgive us our sins and to cleanse us from all
unrighteousness." 1 John 1:9_

Setting the Stage

Most confession of sin starts out with a prayer like this: "Lord, I am *sorry* I yelled at my husband. Please help me do better next time." Or perhaps, "Lord, forgive me for being rude to my co-workers today. I am *really sorry*, I had a rough morning." The funny thing is God never asked for an apology. Let me repeat that: God never said apologize. He said and continues to say *confess your sin*. Nicely packaged apologies are not confessions at all. Apologies may sometimes help you feel better or even calm someone who has been offended, but without touching the spiritual reality that is tied to the confession of sin, they bring no greater power to the Christian life. The truth is we spend too much time apologizing to God when God didn't say apologize. He said "confess."

The word *confession* comes from the translation of the Greek term *homologeo,* which means "to speak or say the

15

same with another, e.g. to say the same thing, to assent to, or be in accord with." When we confess, we are speaking in line with God. We understand and say the same thing about sin that He says. Sounds basic, but what exactly is God saying about sin? Well, it is not just that sin is bad but that He is the remedy for sin: its causes and its effects. Confession of sin speaks to what we lack. It clearly reveals that we have a divine need. Sin proves the absence of God's righteousness influencing a situation. The presence of sin indicates that God does not occupy the proper place in a situation. Confession of sin opens the door for God to enter the situation and give us more of His righteousness. Your life infused with God's righteousness brings you to a place of greater victory and power.

The Power of Confession

Confession of sin is a tool in God's hand, and it is different from an apology. Confession transforms, purifies, and makes way for greater power, strength, and victory in the Christian experience. It causes more of the glory of God to be revealed in and through you. It lifts you to a marvelous manifestation of the fullness of the life of Christ. It cultivates your heart for true expressions of humility, submission, and obedience to the Lord. True confession of sin requires surrender, transparency, reflection, and truth. At first blush, apologizing seems to do the same thing, but it does not produce the same spiritual result. An apology may cover the surface, but it only provides a pseudo healing to the wound. Apologizing for sin fails to address the deeper issues of sin that have marred the soul. Spiritual growth is contingent upon increased understanding of the concept of confession coupled with the practical application of it in your daily life. Understanding and applying the spiritual principles of confession makes way for the realization of a greater demonstration of the power of God in your life. Through this realization, unscriptural patterns can be broken which then catapult you into living your divine purpose.

How did we get confused?

A combination of societal and familial influences has contributed to the belief that apology is the same as a confession. Those influences, though laying a good foundation for social etiquette, caused the formation of a habit that is acceptable to the world but contrary to the principles of God. Let's examine how it all got started, by looking at a familiar childhood event.

Does this scenario sound familiar? As a child you were playing with someone else who had a toy you wanted. So you walked over and took the toy. A chaotic scene ensued. An adult entered the room, and after finding out what was going on they said, "Okay, now you give that toy back and say 'I'm sorry.'" You did what you were told. The other child was told to accept the apology, and of course, they did. You both returned to playing and things seemed to work out fine. The fact that things worked out so well when the words "I'm sorry" were spoken, established a pattern for the rest of your life. You apologize and things get back to normal. The difficulty with this pattern is that it seems to work most of the time, leading you to believe this is the best way. Unfortunately it conditioned you to adopt an unbiblical view in relating to God. The improper thought pattern causes you to treat your confession to God like the apologies given to others. Beware! Social training alone can make you a good citizen of the world but leave you unable to achieve the supernatural benefits of your heavenly citizenship. You must be sure to balance both.

Interestingly enough, the pattern that began as a matter of obedience, set the stage for future behavior when it comes to apologizing. This behavior pattern was probably established long before a decision was made to accept Jesus Christ as

Lord and Savior, which gives a clear indication of why you must challenge its spiritual validity. Decisions, behaviors, and positions established before accepting Christ are clear indicators of the necessity to renew your mind on the subject.

God asked us to confess our sin, and He promised that He would faithfully forgive and cleanse from unrighteousness. Saying "I'm sorry" is not the same as confessing sin, and the effects of an "I'm sorry" do not bring the transformation of your life and faith that confession was designed to do. Absolution not apology precedes spiritual cleansing. Confession is a humbling experience, not a humiliating one. In its divinely therapeutic way, confession brings you closer to God. It provides insight to the work of the Holy Spirit in your life. Confession helps you understand the subsequent dealings of the Holy Spirit. Confession of sin gives rise to repentance because it produces godly sorrow. Godly sorrow produces true repentance that leads to salvation. Only true and proper confession allows you to experience a more intimate relationship with God.

In terms of etiquette, it is important to apologize for actions that offend another person. An apology lets the other person know that you realize a wrong was committed. It helps them. Confession, on the other hand, helps you. The quick "I'm sorry" may be the epitome of social etiquette, but as it relates to God its spiritual yield can sometimes net zero. Quick apologies may make you *feel* absolved of guilt and free to move merrily along but if there is no change in thinking it has been pointless. When it comes to lasting change, inner transformation does not occur without touching Gods reality. Everything in life has its spiritual truth before God. Experiencing God's truth brings you the liberty that Jesus spoke of in John 8:32, *"And you shall know the truth and the truth shall make you free."*

As a spiritually maturing Christian you must become more aware of the reality of the power of confession. It is a foundational requirement for a more effective spiritual walk. They realize confession changes your perspective, your heart, your words, and your actions. Confession changes your life. Let me repeat that. *Confession changes your life.* You can radically change the quality of your life by expanding your thinking in this area. You have the power to transform your Christian walk by allowing the Holy Spirit to renew your mind to God's truth.

In order to increase your spiritual knowledge and grow closer to God, it is essential to view and do things differently. A more spiritual focus is required. Continuing to do things that only touch the physical realm and not the spiritual will cause frustration in your spiritual life. Why do I place so much emphasis on this point? Because living your divine life is at stake. God created you to live powerfully, radically, and abundantly. He has already ordained a life for you that completely glorifies Him and satisfies you. It is important for you to access it, live it, and enjoy it.

It is time to grow and maximize your spiritual walk. Prepare for new thought processes and patterns. A word of caution before we go deeper: apologizing for offenses and showing remorse are necessary behaviors; don't stop those practices. Continue to be good citizens. Just be aware that there is more to life in Christ than cursory apologies when it comes to living powerfully. Let's begin to move from apology to true confession, so that you can reap the spiritual benefits of confession in your life!

From Apology to Confession

Although the task of establishing new patterns of thinking might seem a little daunting, the benefits of the change outweigh any difficulties you might encounter. Making the leap from apology to confession is a powerful step to tearing down the wall that keeps you from a more fulfilling spiritual life. It will increase your power with God and man. It increases your level of intimacy with God and ultimately, the change increases your faith. Not only will you stop offering empty apologies just to smooth things over, but you will also begin to see things from God's perspective. True confession will give you an understanding of His promises, their prerequisites, and their fulfillment in your life. When you learn how to give God what He asks for, you can fully expect to experience His blessing. In order to make the shift you must begin to tear down the wall that stands between you and God's best for your life. Deconstructing the wall begins with addressing a few common myths that keep tend to keep you separated.

Addressing Spiritual Myths

Myth 1: If I say I am sorry then I have confessed my sin

The statement "I am sorry" is an admission of fault while confession of sin is an admission of error. When we have sinned, both fault and error are at work. God is aware that sin is our fault and sets out to correct the error. An apology implies there was a mistake or misdeed, while confession indicates an incorrect belief or philosophy. If you simply offer a surface apology, it only covers the issue of fault.

Quick, haphazard apologies do not touch the reality of God, so they have no power to conquer the affects of sin. An "I'm sorry" does not take into account the Word or the will of God in the situation. It does not come from an understanding of the spiritual problem encountered but a sense of guilt or surface understanding of a mistake. Sometimes, it simply comes out of habit. The continual practice of habitual apology reinforces our belief that this satisfies the will of God when it comes to confession.

Truth 1: Confession of sin reveals error.

Confession is an admission of error; therefore, error is the issue at hand. Error is defined as, "the state of believing what is untrue, incorrect, or wrong." The presence of sin is an indicator of error. Error causes you to miss the mark established by God, which is also the definition of sin. Fault and error travel together and must be dealt with together in order to keep from missing the mark. A mark is a standard. The standards of God are established and meeting them must be the ultimate aim of your life.

When we confess our sin, we are not merely saying, "God, I was wrong" but "I was wrong because my thoughts, words, or actions did not line up with your established standard for the situation." Confession brings us into contact with the will of God. It helps us understand what God's desire is in every situation. Understanding the will of God brings light. When you have light, you are able to walk and work more effectively. Your life's purpose is proving or demonstrating that the will of God is excellent in providing a means to purpose, success, and victorious living. *"And be not conformed to this world, but be ye transformed by the renewing of your mind, that ye may prove what is that good, acceptable, and perfect will of God" Romans 12:2.*

Every situation in our lives touches the will of God. Regardless of the activity, circumstance, or situation, God's will can be known and proven. It is important to recognize your responsibility to demonstrate God's will in all situations. It is more important to be aware that your actions have greater influence than you could have imagined.

Myth 2: If *you* do not accept *my* apology, something is wrong with *you*

Usually offering an apology brings rapid acceptance and a restoration of the relationship. This causes us to believe an apology is like a miracle cure or a magic bullet. It pierces the heart of the person you give it to; bringing them under a power so great, they have to completely accept it. It does not matter that they may have been hurt, angry, disturbed, or offended by the situation. Right? Wrong. Life experience shows us that apologies are sometimes rejected. This rejection offers another indication that there just might be a flaw in system. A flawed system is contrary to the nature of God. God's principles work all the time. They work without fail. The practical application of the principles of God always produces godly results.

When someone rejects an apology and we do not witness the "miracle" of things getting back to "normal," the offended person is typically blamed for being deficient in their social responsibilities. Sometimes a little self-righteousness enters the picture and we feel vindicated believing that they have a bigger problem. The truth is, they just might but the issue at hand is your spiritual walk. *(I could make a great case for a lack of forgiveness here but I'll cover that in another chapter.)* Instead of blaming them or thinking, something is wrong with them, let's take a more spiritual look at the situation.

A person rejects an apology for a multitude of reasons. Sometimes they do not believe it is heartfelt. They have no confidence in the weight of the apology. Other times, they feel the damage caused was deep, and the apologizer just does not get it. It's all connected to forgiveness. Although the rejection of the apology is a serious matter, for now let's just keep in mind the rejection itself shows a flaw in a worldly pattern that can result in spiritual dysfunction.

Truth 2: Confession of sin makes apologies more meaningful

The admission of error and the cleansing work of the Holy Spirit raise the level of your apology exponentially. When you have had a change in perspective and you now see things God's way, the "I'm sorry" comes completely from the heart. David expressed this well in 2 Samuel 12:13, when he declared that his sin was against the Lord with regard to the whole Bathsheba- Uriah fiasco. Psalm 32:5, also reveals that the power of confession, *"I have acknowledged my sin unto thee, and mine iniquity have I not hid. I said, I will confess my transgressions unto the Lord; and thou forgavest the iniquity of my sin."* Confession is required before apology can be offered wholeheartedly. Confession causes you to understand the depths of a situation. Confession paves the road to healing and restoration, not just the apology.

Myth 3: Tears equal repentance

Tears are a response to an emotional trigger, but not all emotional episodes are about repentance. Sometimes people cry simply because they got caught. Tears can also be the result of frustration as the person is not permitted to have their way in a situation. There is a difference between worldly sorrow and godly sorrow. Godly sorrow produces repentance to salvation worldly sorrow leads to death. 2 Corinthians 7:10 says, *"For godly sorrow worketh repentance to salvation not to be repented of: but the sorrow of the world worketh death."* Tears are not an immediate indication of a repentant heart.

Truth 3: You can cry all night and never truly repent

Repentance is only brought on by godly sorrow. Godly sorrow is produced when we no longer view an incident through our perspective but begin to view it through God's perspective. Repentance is "an inward change of mind that produces an outward change of actions." It involves thinking about and doing things the way God would desire. Repentance produces righteousness. If all it took were tears to meet the biblical definition of repentance, Esau would have inherited the blessing he gave up for one morsel of meat. *"For ye know how that afterward, when he would have inherited the blessings, he was rejected: for he found no place of repentance, though he sought it carefully with tears" (Hebrews 12:17).*

Tears are a response to an emotional trigger; therefore, be careful not to confuse tears with repentance.

A New View of Repentance

Growing up, I would often hear people use the word *repent* as a synonym for apology. Someone would say, "Yesterday, I did … and you know I have to repent before Sunday." Even as a child, I would cringe and think that does not make sense. How can you knowingly do wrong and think it's all okay because you planned on "repenting" before Sunday? It had to be more to it than saying, I am sorry. The plan to apologize later did not make it okay, and saying I am sorry surely did not keep them from sinning again. It struck me that somewhere along the way we really believe that simply using the spiritual word *repentance* was enough to make it right. Sounding spiritual does not make your life powerful. A proper understanding and application of repentance moves you into experiencing the divine life.

Godly sorrow produces repentance. Let me repeat the definition of repentance, "a change of mind (inwardly) that produces an outward change of action." True repentance occurs when we see a situation as God sees it, and are impacted by its truth to the point of change. We experience a change in thought, belief, and conduct. Repentance brings our thoughts, beliefs, and actions in line with God's will. Repentance is more than just, "I'm sorry."

It is important to realize that if you are to be free you must get to the root of a problem more than concentrating on the fruit. When you kill the root you kill the tree, and a dead tree cannot produce fruit. The tree rooted in apology and not confession can produce a counterfeit sorrow that might make you think you are in line with God, but lack the effects that godly sorrow produces. Godly sorrow produces repentance. In terms of repentance, not only should you look at the feeling of sorrow but also the effect of that sorrow in terms of what it produces in your life. If it produces a change that lines you up with the will of God then it has been profitable. If it produces a change that moves you away from the will of God, it has been unprofitable. *"Now I rejoice, not that ye were made sorry, but that ye sorrowed to repentance: for ye were made sorry after a godly manner, that ye might receive damage by us in nothing. For godly sorrow worketh repentance to salvation not to be repented of: but the sorrow of the world worketh death"* (2 Corinthians 7:9-10).

Repentance is an integral part of your worship experience. If worship is bowing or becoming obedient to the will of another then accepting God's perspective on an issue and living in line with that view is an act of worship. The denial of your own will (thoughts, reasoning, and justifications) and the accepting of God's will creates a closer relationship between you and the Father, which is an awesome benefit of worship.

A true change in thinking leads to a change in behavior. It causes you to become a more faithful follower of God, which in turn, makes you a formidable opponent to the kingdom of darkness. It lifts you to new levels of influence and effectiveness as a Kingdom expander. There is nothing more powerful than a holy life. A life God can use for His purpose. A holy life truly glorifies His name by understanding and honoring His Word. The key to unlocking all this in your life is unlocking greater spiritual truth about confession and repentance.

Repentance and confession, confession and repentance either way you say it, go hand and hand. There is no repentance without thoughtful consideration of the Word of God. There is no confession without thoughtful consideration of the Word of God and an acceptance of the work of the Holy Spirit in your life.

Eradicating a skewed vision of repentance is essential. True repentance causes change, and that change should be evident in your daily life. The Holy Spirit works in your life to ensure that you become more and more like Christ, and uniquely fulfill God's purposes as a result of healthy confession and true repentance. So how do you get to the true repentance that produces change and increases your life fulfillment? It begins when you embrace God's truth about confession and abandon futile apologies.

Keys to Understanding True Spiritual Confession
The Issue of Lack

Confession of sin involves an understanding of lack. If you can grab hold of this truth, it will be transform your life. Confession of sin works hand-in-hand with repentance. The issue of sin reveals the absence of something in the life of a believer. The lack that sin reveals is unbelief. Most people are challenged by the thought that sin is ultimately the result of unbelief. Nevertheless, it is true. Unbelief is the root of all sin. The spiritual work of confession breaks the chains of sin resulting from unbelief, and releases strength and power in your spiritual walk.

God has desires for us; lack and unbelief are not in His plan. Our lack of belief and experience is not the fault of God. God desires us to have complete belief in Him and all that He says to us through His Word. He wants our experience on Earth to be one of victory, power, and purpose. His desire is that we experience the supernatural benefits of confession. We must fulfill His purpose and to that end He gives us all that we need. Confession is about maturing in faith and wisdom. It is about receiving God's supply to meet our need.

At conversion, you were given the seed of the fruit of the Spirit. This seed is to grow to maturity producing all that God requires. Confession is one of the catalysts of our maturational process. It acts like fertilizer in that it kills the things that choke the growth of the seed. Improper confession can delay our spiritual growth and development. Confession invites the Holy Spirit in to cleanse and purify us. This cleansing is actually the second component of the "confess-forgive" continuum. Cleansing is the result of true confession. Cleansing is required, without it, we sin again. Your enemy would have you think that apology is the same as confession and to ignore the fact that confession brings purification. Purity is power. Your confession connects you with Gods desire. It gives Him an opportunity to help you.

The Work of the Holy Spirit

Once we confess our sin, we are poised for the Holy Spirit to work on us. The Holy Spirit's function regarding confession is to cleanse us from all unrighteousness. The cleansing takes place through a myriad of functions. Of course, when we look at cleansing biblically, we find that the agents of cleansing are typically fire, water, and the Word. The Holy Spirit will cleanse us through each or all of these means. The Word is the catalytic agent that propels the cleansing, but we must be aware that God uses situations, circumstances, tests, and trials to bring us to the place where we are moving in confidence and suffer no lack in our faith toward His ability in us.

The Holy Spirit knows best what to bring into our lives to accomplish the task the Father has given Him. For example, if you have discovered that your inability to change is due to your lack of trust in the Lord, you can rest assured that the Holy Spirit will lead you into situations that allow your trust to increase. The Holy Spirit will cleanse you from all unrighteousness and cause the righteousness of God to be revealed through you.

Erroneous thinking in sacred and secular arenas has also contributed to the development of a behavior pattern that separates us from the power of true faith, yielding a harvest of ineffective living. Any process, pattern, or way of living that denies the power and right of God in your life is hazardous to your faith. Any doctrine, tradition, or method that denies

God's power, ability, or sovereignty over your life is detrimental to your spiritual growth. We see this in the instances of positive thinking or positive confession. There is nothing inherently wrong with a positive attitude or speaking positive words but they should be based on God's truth. If the thought or words deny or limit God's truth, it is an affront to God's sovereignty.

Ironically, sometimes we are so consumed with not making a negative confession that we lie to ourselves and block the power of God from moving in our lives. For example, if you have a headache, it is real. You do not deny it. You do not have to say things that sound spiritual but have no power. The fact is, you have a headache, yet the greater truth is that Jesus is the one who heals. Therefore, I confess my need and He is faithful to meet the need. Jesus said, "I came for the sick; those who are well have no need for a physician." He spoke to us on all levels—spiritual, emotional, and physical. So we must begin to really evaluate the truth of our statements and what they reveal.

You should remember that "missing the mark" is the definition of sin. So, what causes people to miss the mark? It is unbelief, plain and simple. All occurrences of sin have a traceable line of unbelief. In almost every situation, the thread of unbelief can be followed to the outward manifestation of sin. When a spouse is unfaithful, there is unbelief about what God says about marriage, the individual life, and the consequences of disobedience. The violation of divine truth can be connected to any or all of those points. When a child is disobedient or dishonors their parents, there is unbelief about what God says about the rewards of honoring and obeying parents, the consequences of disobedience, or the role of authority in their lives. Again, the violation of divine truth can stem from one or all of these issues. If left at the level of confessing the action and not identifying the root of unbelief only temporary change will occur. Temporarily turning from sin only to return does not speak of true conversion. True conversion is demonstrated through the permanent change in the heart, belief, and actions. The heart issue must be sufficiently managed. Belief eradicates sin, converts and cleanses the soul, and produces an upright walk before God.

How then do we deal with the heart issue? It begins with honestly facing the truth. The truth that needs to be faced is that unbelief is present. This is a hard point for believers to apprehend. Most people think that once they have believed in Christ there is no longer any unbelief in them but this would negate the ministry of the Holy Spirit. The Holy Spirit works in us and through us to bring us to the pure demonstration of holiness and righteousness. Even though it may be difficult to confess there is unbelief to grow strong spiritually, you must press forward. One remarkable point about identifying and overcoming unbelief is that it is uniquely tied to the concept of lack. Specifically, it is tied to our perceived lack that we try to fill outside of God. Confession of sin then becomes a way to identify unbelief, which in turn becomes a way to discover what we lack in our lives.

Speaking in line with God requires that you are transparent about missing the mark. Recognizing the root of sin and facing the harsh reality that it identifies an area of lack positions you to avoid future sin. You can only truly evaluate the root of sin against the Word of God through the illumination of the Holy Spirit. Diligent prayer, study of the Scripture along with obedient execution of the principles of the word will give you greater understanding of the perceived lack in your life that caused you to sin. This understanding gives you the power to repent. Repentance is to have a change of mind that results in a change of belief and actions. When true repentance has occurred you do things God's way. Pleasing God and living powerfully become automatic and not burdensome.

Ultimately, it is important to understand that God does not desire that we suffer lack. He came that we might have abundant life. Our proper confession of sin reveals that life.

The concepts of unbelief and perceived lack may be foreign to your way of thinking yet the work and ministry of the Holy Spirit fully supports them. When we confess sin, God is faithful and just to forgive us and to cleanse us from unrighteousness, right? If righteousness can be explained as right beliefs that generate right actions, unrighteousness can be explained as incorrect beliefs that cause improper actions. The incorrect belief then has to stem from ignorance of the truth in the word of God or the failure to make the connection between your actions and God's truth. Ignorance of the truth in the word of God does not mean that one has no ability to read, understand, but it speaks of the lack of experience with the truth that comes from obedience and the work of the Holy Spirit. The Holy Spirit comes to help uncover error and fill us with truth as well as illuminate the Scripture. His presence makes the word of God pure, practical, and powerful. Suppose you get into an argument with someone. After the argument, you feel bad and apologize to them for the incident. Everything with the person seems to be fine but you still are not over it. Later when you enter into a time of prayer, you talk to God about what happened; the argument, the pain, the unkind words, the hurt feelings, etc. you ask for forgiveness. You can certainly be forgiven but suppose you not only talk to him about the argument but also about your thoughts, feelings, and actions. When you begin to communicate with God on this level, you will begin to ask, "Why I reacted that way?" or "Why did this happen?" or an even better question might be, "How can I honor your name in every situation?" As you begin to communicate on a deeper level, you open the door for cleansing. When you recognize that, you can exercise power in every situation you will begin to seek God to know of the power contained in His word that you need in order to live for Him. It is at this point that you have made shift from seeking absolution from the difficult circumstance to deliverance from the root of the action.

What Are You Really Confessing?

To this point, things have been deeply spiritual. Yet, the ability to translate the deeply spiritual to powerful, practical application is to really prove God's will on earth. Let's take a look at what might be lacking in your belief as you confess certain things to God. This will help you identify lack in your own life.

Frustration. When your confession to God is that you are frustrated, the spiritual reality before God may be tied to a lack of love, faith, or patience.

Frustration that develops because of a lack of love occurs when you are unable to realize your desires because there is an unmet expectation. This type of frustration is typically evident in relationships. The challenge here is that the unmet expectation may be real or perceived. It can also be spoken or unspoken. The ability to deal with our expectations in a godly manner is important. The writings of Galatians teach us that there is a proper way for handling unmet expecta- tions- talk about them to the offending party. Operating in the love of God does not mean you have no standards, but the power of God working in you never produces frustration and destruction. Rather, it teaches you to handle all situa- tions with grace and poise. If your standard is set by your own will, desires, or feelings and not in line with the will of God, you will become frustrated. In order to overcome this lack you must align your beliefs, thinking, and action with God's will.

Frustration that develops as a lack of faith is usually revealed in work or goal oriented situations. When you are blocked from accomplishing something because it seems that doors are being slammed shut or perhaps people are not being cooperative. It is important to rely on your faith and the reality that God knows exactly what is going on in your life at every given moment. You must be completely persuaded that He is working even when it seems things have come to a standstill. You must place your trust in His ability to meet your needs and work through you. In order to overcome this type of frustration you must recognize that God is the creative authority of heaven and earth. If you need a new way to think, act or move it must come from Him.

Frustration developing from a lack of patience is commonly displayed in actions and attitudes towards others. This too, ties in with the concept of love. 1 Corinthians 13 tells us that love is patient and kind. When impatience and short temperedness rear its head, it simply reveals that there is a lack of love. Here you must practice demonstrating greater grace, compassion, and poise. Let's look at another common area of confession and its corresponding lack.

Anger. When you confess anger, the reality before God is not that you got angry. God knows that you will at times become angry. In fact, anger is a characteristic of God. The issue is not that you stop getting angry but that anger is precipitated by the correct force. More often than not, believers become angry because of a violation of their own personal will, desires, and emotions. The spiritually strong believer is slow to anger because they know a violation of the will of God produces righteous anger not merely a reaction to their hurt feelings. When you confess anger you must keep in mind that anger comes because of something happening to you that was not desired. So, then confessing anger is not about anger at all but the stimulus that caused the anger. Some common triggers for anger are feeling disrespected, belittled, ignored, neglected, or unloved. Each of these can be tied to the lack of meekness or perhaps, temperance.

Power under control is the best definition of meekness. The person who exhibits meekness is one who is confident in their level of power and authority. They are enlightened about their own identity. The conflict comes when someone else violates your power or authority. Anger is typically the undesired response to such violations. The lack may be that you are unsure of who you are and the power you have therefore you feel the need to fight for it. This is not God's way. God who has all power suffers abuses and slights to his power and authority everyday but they do not diminish who he is. He is God. If we are made in His image and His likeness then we suffer abuses and slights to our power and authority we do not have to lose our cool but can proceed with love, compassion, grace, and mercy. Meekness travels with temperance, which is self-control. If your lack involves meekness, there is usually a lack of self-control or discipline as well. The meek person handles offenses and affront in a godly manner. He handles these things in a manner that is led by the Holy Spirit and not his own mind, will, or emotions. When this lack is at the root of anger, the Holy Spirit goes to work to develop greater meekness and self-control.

How God responds to your lack

Acknowledging unbelief begins the powerful process of spiritual cleansing. In fact, until unbelief is acknowledged there is only a temporary fix to the situation, which can result in a painful cycle of repetitious acts. The powerful results of confession are obtained when unbelief is acknowledged. This acknowledgment gives way for us to identify that lack in our lives. When our lack is clearly revealed, God is able to fill us with His righteousness. His righteousness obliterates our tendency for recidivism.

At the heart of unbelief is a perceived lack. When you acknowledge unbelief you must then ask the question, "What is it that I don't believe?" At the root of all unbelief is a perception of lack. It is not enough to simply say, "God forgive me for my unbelief." You should identify what it is that you don't believe. This might be a difficult step because it will cause you to come face to face with the holiness of God. It is however, a much needed step because it gives you clarity on the issues of your heart. It reveals what you need from God but are not persuaded that He will supply it. It reveals that you may have attempted to find another way to meet that need. God is the supplier of all you need. If there is a need that you have God is able to fill it. The challenge comes when we try to fill the need ourselves. When God fills a need it will never violate His principles. Your need will be continually satisfied. More often than not, God's principles are violated when we try to fill our own needs. Man's attempts at self-fulfillment violate the main principle of worship because it causes him to dismiss the dominion and authority of God. The Bible clearly teaches that we are to have no other gods before God, that we should have dominion over all things, and that as believers we stand in the delegated authority of Jesus Christ. Trying to fill your own need without respect for the will of God actually opens the door for other things to control you. When God is not the master of your life, you live beneath the power and privilege originally intended. You fall prey to the power and authority of other gods, which can never truly satisfy. It is important to embrace the fact that God gave Himself as the supply for all of our needs. He provides everything you need for a successful and satisfying life. Always trust and depend on Him. It is His will and His desire for you. Your spiritual walk will continuously become more purposeful and powerful when your will and desires line up with God's will. As God supplies all your need, the reality of the cleansing work of the Holy Spirit becomes apparent in your life.

On an even more practical note, say you have a problem with smoking. You have tried to quit for some time, and it causes problems in your relationships. Now it is starting to cause a problem in your prayer times. You can't get through them without needing to take a smoke break. So you decide to give up the habit. Yet in times of stress and strain you find yourself smoking again, only now you hide it from everyone, even God. You are consumed with guilt, and so you go to God and confess your sin. From your perspective, cigarettes are your nemesis; the terrible thing you need deliverance from and while that may be true there is the view from God's perspective. From God's perspective, you have not trusted in His ability to carry you through every situation. You have become dependent upon something other than the Word and power of God to bring you comfort, peace, and refreshing. This is the problem before God. He has ordained that the very thing you need is provided to you through the Holy Spirit. See, the thing that God begins to cleanse you from is a lack of trust. Confession of sin and cleansing always connects us to recognizing our lack. Think about the account of the fall from the book of Genesis:

> "Now the serpent was more crafty than any beast of the field which the Lord God had made. And he said to the woman, "Indeed, has God said, 'You shall not eat from any tree of the garden'?" And the woman said to the serpent, "From the fruit of the trees of the garden we may eat; but from the fruit of the tree which is in the middle of the garden, God has said, 'You shall not eat from it or touch it, lest ye die.'" And the serpent said to the woman, "You surely shall not die! For God knows that in the day that you eat from it your eyes will be opened, and **you will be like God, knowing good and evil.**" When the woman saw that the tree was good for food, and that it was a delight to the eyes, and **that the tree was desirable to make one wise,** she took from its fruit and ate;

and she gave also to her husband with her, and he ate." Genesis 3:1-5

Though there are many teaching points from these few lines of text, I have emphasized the one most important here as it relates to confession and lack. Eve believed that she lacked something. The thing she believed she lacked was wisdom. The moment she began to believe she lacked something, it gave way to the commission of sin. It wasn't a matter of food, because she could get food from the other trees. It wasn't a matter of what she did have but what she thought she did not have. Our sin is often the result of an attempt to get something we believe we do not already possess.

As a redeemed believer, always realize that you are complete in Christ and have been given all things for life and godliness. Unrighteousness causes us to think we must obtain something through our own strength, power, or might. Eve thought she was missing an essential ingredient in her existence, and that was the beginning of the end.

The problem with man comes from the same root: God has supplied everything but we do not truly believe it. God has ordained a process and plan for accomplishing His will, and we must be in line with it. All we have to do is follow the plan—exhibit righteousness, which is proper actions, based on proper speaking that precipitates from proper thinking. We must come to understand that God truly loves us and wants the best for us. Any prohibitions from the Lord should be viewed as a means to unlock greater liberty and provide protection. God wants us to enjoy life and bring Him pleasure by appreciating all that He has done for us.

Imparting Spiritual Truth

Saying "I'm sorry" causes a temporary sense of absolution, yet it lacks the power to keep you from repeating the same offense. This sets up a never-ending cycle of sin, guilt, apology, relief, sin, guilt, and apology. Can you see how a seemingly innocent pattern established in our lives can produce a cycle of bondage?

God does not just want to forgive your sin; He wants you to experience the victory that comes from that forgiveness. The Holy Spirit is the agent that works on and in you to accomplish the manifestation of God's will for your life. If we do not confess sin but continue to apologize, His help is limited. Life becomes an exercise of living by sheer willpower and not the power of the Holy Spirit. Living by your own willpower guarantees that at some point you will fail, but living by God's power guarantees complete, total, and eternal victory.

God's statement was clear and concise: confess your sin and He will forgive and cleanse you. Rid your life of prayers that are filled with apologies and excuses that soothe your conscience but do not purify your soul. God knows that you are sorry about the things you have done. The hard truth is that you don't get credit for being sorry unless it produces repentance. *"For godly sorrow worketh repentance to salvation not be repented of: but the sorrow of the world worketh death" (2 Corinthians 7:10).*

Confession is powerful and God would not tell us to do something if there was no divine effect attached to it. God is committed to His purpose and you are a part of that. In order to accomplish God's purposes your life must be more and more in line with His will. He has no interest in you remaining the same, but His desire is for you to reflect His image back toward Him and to reveal His. You were created to function in the earth like a prism: receiving the power and perfection of God's light and refracting it into the earth to subdue, replenish, and increase godliness.

Confession is a powerful reminder that God is light. In Him, there is no darkness. Sin in us is darkness, and once we have discovered it and confessed it to Him; He forgives us and removes the darkness, replacing it with light. If we have rightly confessed and not merely apologized, we will be filled with light and not return to the sin again.

Confession serves as a catalyst for the movement of the Holy Spirit in you. Remember our focal verse, 1 John 1:9: *"If we confess our sin, he is faithful and just to forgive us our sin and to cleanse us from all unrighteousness."* Forgiveness is the work of God and cleansing the operation of God through the Holy Spirit. The two-fold statement indicates that in the mind of God, some dirtiness or filth is associated with our sin. He wants to eradicate it. We are to be cleansed from those things that are not in line with God in thought, principle, or deed. Therefore, we are to be forgiven of sin and cleansed of everything that prohibits us from meeting God's standard. Most of the time when we think of sin, we are concerned with forgiveness of a certain behavior, yet its scope includes thoughts and attitudes. Behavior is the product of thoughts and beliefs. For us to only deal with the behavior aspect of it leaves of void of the complete truth. God's concern is for the beliefs that lead to the action. Missing the mark is a heart issue. It is the inward rejection of a divine truth not simply an outward action. Jesus, said, *"Ye have heard it said by them of old time, Thou shalt not commit adultery: But I say unto you, that whosoever looketh on a woman to lust after her hath committed adultery with her already in his heart."* Some would believe that until an actual physical act is committed that sin has not occurred yet the words of Jesus leave no room for doubt that action is the final display of rebellion because the departure from righteousness occurred at the place of the heart.

When you identify and acknowledge the violation of divine truth, you will experience true victory. You will experience the profound richness of forgiveness and the renewal of spiritual cleansing. This may be a new way of thinking about sin and confession but the ability to get to the fundamental truth opens up a spiritual pathway that leads to a more dynamic Christian walk. This pathway can only be discovered when you allow the Holy Spirit to change your perspective of concept.

From man's perspective, the request for forgiveness is about getting out of a sticky situation or the desire to feel better. From God's perspective, it is about restoring righteousness. He is the supplier of all our need. He gives us everything. God fills us because it equips us to accomplish His purpose. He does not desire that we suffer lack. He supplies all our need according to His riches in glory. God wants to fill us with the light of who He is. He wants to fill us with truth, power, and love that we may fulfill His mandate in the earth. We must align ourselves with God, not allowing darkness to dwell in us by way of unconfessed sin. Unconfessed sin causes us to live beneath the level of privilege and power He designed for us. Confession of sin then becomes such an important part of spiritual growth that we must be certain to consistently apply the principles in our lives, always speaking in line with God.

When we speak in line with God about sin, we must keep a few things in mind. First, God despises sin and cannot look upon it. Second, the wages of sin is death. As believers, however, we have already accepted Jesus and believe in the power of His death and resurrection to free us from the penalty of sin. This is only one aspect of salvation. As recipients of God's gift of salvation, we are assured daily assistance from the dominion and effects of sin in our lives. Unconfessed sin can keep you from living a life in the fullness that God designed. It hinders your usefulness in the kingdom. Ultimately, it can come down to a salvation issue.

Finally, it is important to recognize that confession of sin has the connotation of conceding. Concession means admitting that I have been wrong and you have been right. One concedes in the face of irrefutable facts. When a candidate runs for office and at the close of polls on election night, when it becomes evident that they cannot win, they concede the election. The surrender to the empirical data evidenced by the counting of votes causes the opponent to give up and offer support to the other. Our confession is the same. We must see from the empirical data of the Word, our actions, and consequences that we have been wrong and God has been right. We must learn to concede.

Bridging the Gap

Since a confession is not the same as an apology, and God didn't say apologize, it makes sense that an improper understanding of this fact produces improper action, which creates a spiritual disconnection between us and the power of the Holy Spirit. Bridging the gap between where we are and where God wants us to be happens as we employ the following steps:

- Desire God's wisdom and forgiveness
- Understand the spiritual reality behind missing the mark
- Surrender to the work of the Holy Spirit
- Receive God's impartation of truth and righteousness regarding the situation
- Walk in newness of life and victory

Remember that confession of sin requires the power of God to help you see the truth behind missing the mark. Stop apologizing to God and *confess* as He requires, that you may touch the reality of sin and be cleansed of all unrighteousness. Confession is the believer's responsibility before God. He desires that you fully experience the power that comes as a result of His work in you and through you.

God declares that He wants to do a new thing in you, that He *will* do a new thing in you. He erased the old, and all things have become new. That is license to rid yourself of old patterns, habits, and behaviors. You must relinquish those patterns, habits, and behaviors that are positive as well as those that are dysfunctional. God, through the work of the Holy Spirit, wants to renew your mind and transform your life. Cling tightly to the Word of God, apply it in accordance with His truth, and allow the Holy Spirit to work in you.

Start the process of erasing old habits and allowing new, empowering patterns to be established in your life. *"And be not conformed to this world: but be ye transformed by the renewing of your mind, that ye may prove what is that good and acceptable and perfect will of God." Romans 12:2*

Take some time and examine whether your life has been one of apologies. If you have been apologizing, review the words of this chapter along with referenced scriptures, and begin to confess.

Let's Pray:

Father, I confess that I have given too many apologies and too few confessions of sin. I ask You now in the name of Jesus to forgive me and from this point on to guide me through Your Holy Word to true confessions that release the power of the Holy Spirit in my life. I thank You for renewing my mind and transforming my life, that I may indeed prove the good, perfect, and acceptable will of God. I love You and pray in faith. Amen.

Renew Your Mind...

Think about the previous chapter. What challenged your thinking in this area? Take a moment and interact with the material by journaling your thoughts prior to reading and your thoughts now.

_____

_____

_____

_____

_____

_____

_____

_____

_____

Transform Your Walk...

Change occurs when we move from thinking to doing. Change involves action. What have you been apologizing to God about that you need to confess? List those things, recalling the definition of confession, and allow the Holy Spirit to take you deeper so that you will begin to understand what God has to say about the issue.

_____

_____

_____

_____

_____

_____

_____

_____

_____

Chapter Two

God Didn't Say...
There Would Be No Consequences

*"Before I was afflicted I went astray:
but now have I kept thy word." Psalm 119:67*

Setting the Stage

I am forgiven. Praise God! Hallelujah! But why do I have to deal with the effects of my actions? They are painful and sometimes grievous. The fact of the matter is while God is faithful and just to forgive us our sin and cleanse us from all unrighteousness, consequences still result from our actions. We must be ready and willing to experience them. Somehow we tend to tie forgiveness of sin with the obliteration of consequences, and *God Didn't Say That!* God never said forgiveness erases consequences. The belief that consequences are obliterated with an apology actually has its roots in a childhood game.

Do you remember playing truth or consequences as a child? The object of the game was to tell the truth about a question to avoid punitive consequences from your friends. The purpose of the game was to get you to reveal some valuable details about your life. If you refused, you had to endure whatever actions the game captain desired to inflict. Since the object of the game was to get you to reveal truth, the consequences were usually horrible. Most of the time the consequences were embarrassing or gross—like running around the block barking like a dog or eating some terrible combination of food. The captain was able to require obedience and inflict pain based entirely on his or her own inclinations. Essentially, when you played the game you listened to the question and decided whether you would answer the question or pay the consequences.

The interesting thing about playing this game was that if the question was too personal, you *could* elect to take the consequences instead of revealing the truth. The problem here is that the game leads one to believe that all consequences are optional. Many believers think consequences are under their own power and all they have to do is tell the truth to avert consequences. This creates so many challenges to spiritual growth. Unlike the childhood game of truth or consequences, life is not an either/or situation.

The either/or mentality is destructive to our faith walk. Thinking that it is either truth or consequences positions us for an inaccurate view of God. Believing, even on a subconscious level, that our confession removes consequences will cause disappointment and possibly even doubt about our salvation and standing in Christ. These feelings take us on a journey God never intended us to travel. Erroneous thinking about consequences can cause you to doubt that God has accepted you and loves you. Doubts about God's love for you can keep you from experiencing the fullness of the fruit of salvation in your life. Doubts about salvation can produce a life of diminishing faith and little power. The faulty thoughts about consequences cause you to create a false reality. The belief that once I confess to God everything will be fine does not provide a firm foundation when life happens. Experiencing consequences can abruptly shake your faith. Confession does not remove the consequences of bad choices. God never promised there would be no consequences. The Bible repeatedly shows that consequences are the result of actions. Whether we love God or have no regard for Him, consequences are a part of life.

Consequences are by nature designed to kill you. There are times when the consequences of our actions produce natural death, but spiritual death is the more the point of this discussion. Although consequences are designed to kill you, the beauty of it is that you as a believer can survive the consequences. The ability to endure consequences and prevail to righteousness is your living testimony to the world that God is with you. Your testimony is that with Christ you prevail over all things. Life in Christ means, consequences cannot kill you. The thing that separates you from the world is not the alleviation of consequences or the removal of trials but the presence of the Lord with you. The reality of His presence is evidenced by your continued obedience in the midst of the storm.

Even after this explanation, many believers will not embrace this fact; they will hold tightly to the belief that if they tell God the truth there will be no consequences. Although they profess to agree with this point, their actions in the face of consequences tell a different story. The acceptance of truth is revealed through actions, not mental understanding. The experience of truth is not solely intellectual—it is more than mental assent. The disparity between our thoughts and the truth is further evidence of our desire to have consequences disappear. It is important to deal with the inward desire that still exists, the desire that shows up in the form of a prayer begging God to take the consequences away. God is well able to avert consequences, and in His mercy He may do so, but it should not be the prevailing sentiment of our heart.

God purposely designed and ordained consequences. His plans are not our plans. His ways are not our ways. When it comes to consequences we must remember He knows what's best for us. His promise is not that we will always be insulated against things happening but that He will always be there. If growth in faith and living are the aim, then a clear understanding of the role of consequences in our lives must be obtained. Understanding this point will help us demonstrate our confidence in God even in the face of difficult circumstances. For if God is truly for us who can be against us?

Consequences and Forgiveness

Forgiveness does not erase consequences. Experiencing consequences in your life does not mean you are not forgiven. Forgiveness and consequences are mutually exclusive concepts in the economy of God.

Forgiveness is a merciful and gracious act of God. It is defined theologically as "pardon for sin." A pardon is a legal term denoting a release from the legal penalties of an offense. When we receive God's forgiveness, we are released from the legal penalty of our sin, which is death. Romans 6:23 states, *"for the wages of sin is death but the free gift of God is eternal life in Christ Jesus our Lord."* However, forgiveness does not end the civil effect that results from that sin. Consider this: a young couple engages in premarital sex and the young woman becomes pregnant. She comes to know Christ, repents of her previous actions, and finds her place in the family of God. She is completely forgiven of her sin. Death is no longer required for what she has done. She is no longer cut off from God but can have communion and fellowship with Him. Yet the child she had does not go away. In fact, the woman may experience many challenges as a result of the act she committed, but it does not nullify her state of being forgiven. She is forgiven. The consequences and challenges of life are the result of choices made, but true fellowship with God is evidence of receiving His forgiveness. The only way to deal with the consequences is to submit to the will of God and apply the life-giving principle of the Word. This might be a strong example, but its relevance supports the point that forgiveness does not obliterate consequences. It actually opens another door for us to extend our faith and trust in Jesus Christ.

King David, a man after God's own heart, experienced difficult consequences in his life. The type of consequences he endured might have taken out the best of them, but because of his choices through the consequences, he was able to realize God's faithfulness. David's life had its share of mistakes, missteps, and sometimes just plain bad decisions; yet he still reigned as king, won many battles, and enjoyed the favor of the Lord. His life was not perfect and he often endured the consequences of his actions. By experiencing those consequences he came to know God in a deeper and more meaningful way.

We can learn a lot from David about the power of God's forgiveness. David's ability to maintain a proper attitude about consequences coupled with his heartfelt repentance kept him on the path of his divine destiny and secured God's favor in his life. He demonstrated the beauty of remaining faithful to God in good times and bad. If we look closer at David's missteps and the consequences he endured we can understand God better. By patterning our response to consequences after David's responses, our trust and passion toward God will be increased. David shows us that above consequences there must be a passionate love for God and a reverent respect for His authority over our lives. Our ability to follow his example will solidify our walk. It is important to maintain a heart of love and a posture of worship before the Lord at all times. Let's take a closer look at how to handle consequences from the life of David.

David and Bathsheba

David, God's anointed and divinely chosen king of Israel, had an affair with a woman named Bathsheba. The affair produced a child; when David became aware of that, he arranged an elaborate cover-up that failed. After the initial cover-up failed, David orchestrated a plan that would lead to Bathsheba's husband being killed in battle. It worked. David and Bathsheba were married and she gave birth to a child. Everything appeared to be going smoothly for the king. He managed to hide his sin from everyone and obtained what he wanted, yet there was one he could not hide his sin from and that was God. God spoke to Nathan the prophet and Nathan spoke to David. Although David was knee-deep in denial and trying to live a normal life, his psalms give us a clear indication that he was not at ease with what he had done. Once confronted by Nathan, David confessed his sin and received forgiveness from the Lord. He was forgiven, yet he would face consequences that lasted a lifetime. Let's take a closer look at the Scripture:

> Thus said the Lord, Behold, I will raise up evil against thee out of thine own house and will take thy wives before thine eyes, and give them unto thy neighbor, and he shall live with thy wives in the sight of the sun. For thou didst it secretly: but I will do this thing before all Israel and before the sun. And David said unto Nathan, I have sinned against the Lord. And Nathan said unto David, the Lord also hath put away thy sin: thou shalt not die. Howbeit, because by this deed thou has given great occasion to the enemies of the Lord to blaspheme, the child also that is born unto thee shall surely die.
>
> 2 Samuel 12:11-14

Wow! David's consequences were severe. God meted out the consequences of David's actions: family turmoil, loss of relationships, and the loss of the child. David's life would have to bear the consequences of his actions. They would be uncomfortable, embarrassing, and painful. Yet God through Nathan said, "Thou shalt not die." When we read it today, it might seem like little consolation, but the truth that statement contains is far weightier. God promised David that through all he had to endure he would not die. It might be rough, but you will live. You will cry, but you will live. People may think they are prevailing over you, but you will live. It won't always be easy, but you will live. You will suffer loss, but you will live. God's love and power are the only things that can protect you from the outcome that consequences are designed to produce in your life. Forgiveness is a kingdom key that opens the door to life. Experiencing God's forgiveness insulates you from the impending death that consequences are designed to produce.

The consequences of his actions would have long-term effects. The timing of the consequences and their duration was not under David's control. God didn't set up a timeframe for when all the consequences would come to an end. Have you ever been in a place where the consequences seemed like they would never come to an end? You must act as David acted. He maintained a heart of worship regardless of the consequences. David was forgiven but not absolved of the consequences.

Like many of us, I can imagine that David had no idea his actions would lead to all that. Like many of us, David probably wanted things to be over quickly. This is not always God's way. We do not decide how long consequences last, nor do we determine whether they are too harsh. We can only recognize as David did that we sinned against God and our fate must therefore lie with God. David put his trust in the faithfulness and righteous judgment of God. He was obvi-

ously overtaken with the temporary pleasures of self-gratification. Consider the facts of David's situation when you
are about to make a decision. Consider that your actions can
open a floodgate of consequences that will affect your life
for years to come. The inherent gravity of that point should
cause us to develop a higher regard for the choices we make.
We can also learn that no man is an island and our decisions
produce ripple effects.

The death of David and Bathsheba's son might seem to
be the ultimate price to pay in consequences, but even in that
we can learn a great deal about the role of consequences in
our life. The severity of the judgment shows that our position in Christ does not keep us from harsh penalties when our
actions demand it. Additionally, from the example of David
we learn that consequences are not always swift or have a
short lifespan. There are limitations to them, but those limitations are governed by the Word of God not our desire. Man
desires to see a quick end to unpleasantness, but that is not
always God's way. The effects of actions will continue until
they have arrived at their divinely purposed end. The end to
all consequences, or the effects of sin, is death. Consequences
are by nature designed to drive you farther and farther away
from God. Consequences are designed to kill you.

Consequences Are Designed to Kill You

Yes, it is a radical statement, but look at the definition of
the word *consequence*. A consequence as defined by Merriam
Webster's online dictionary is "something produced by a
cause or necessarily following from a set of conditions."
In other words it is an action, group of actions, or series of
events that are the result of activity both active and passive.

In the beginning of time God gave Adam a mandate.
He told him that he could eat from every tree of the garden
except the tree of the knowledge of good and evil. Adam by
all accounts had it made. God told Adam that on the day he

ate from this tree a consequence would follow—he would surely die. *"And the Lord God commanded the man, saying, Of every tree of the garden thou mayest freely eat: But of the tree of the knowledge of good and evil, thou shalt not eat of it: for in the day that thou eatest thereof thou shalt surely die"* *(Genesis 2:16-17).* Essentially what He said was, when you disobey Me and eat of the tree, a series of events will take place that produce death. The series of events can also be called consequences. The Lord did not give any specifics on what death would look like, taste like, or feel like in experience; He simply said that man would die. Death was the only thing guaranteed as a result of disobedience. So, following the same line of reasoning, when we commit acts contrary to God's will, death becomes an imminent byproduct of those actions. Remember Romans 6:23? *"For the wages of sin is death but the gift of God is eternal life through Jesus Christ our Lord."* Consequences are designed to kill you, but God's gift of eternal life nullifies the final outcome.

Although consequences are designed to kill you, death does not have to come immediately. God wasn't in a hurry then and He isn't in a hurry now, so consequences don't have to be immediate in their manifestation. God dwells in the realm of eternity. Time is in our realm not His. So He can let things run their full course of action regardless of how long it seems to take. The Bible tells us that God's Word shall not return to Him empty or unfulfilled, but it will produce the results He desires and prosper in the object that He sends it to. God allows consequences to be completed knowing that His Word is true and the power of it will remain.

Genesis 3:19 states, *"In the sweat of thy face shalt thou eat bread, **till** thou return unto the ground; for out of it wast thou taken: for dust thou art, and unto dust shalt thou return."* Sometimes the process of experiencing consequences is a slow erosion of life. The judgment from Genesis 3 shows that the effects of consequences will be seen in your spiri-

51

tual life, physical life, and material life. Spiritually, death is separation from God. If God is life and the source of all life, then to be separated from Him is to be virtually without a power source. Just as a piece of electronic equipment void of a power source becomes useless, likewise a human being separated from the source of life and energy becomes useless in fulfilling their divine purpose on earth. Second, to be separated from the presence of God is like an ice cube being out of the freezer—after a while it melts.

Consequences affect your physical life. God cursed the ground after Adam and Eve sinned. The curse made work toilsome for them. The ground that had been created to produce easily and freely under the command of God would now need to be worked with sweat and strain to obtain fruit from it. Work would require much more of man's energy and time, and anything man gained would only come through sweat and toil. Excessive labor wears down the body and eventually leads to death. Not only does excessive labor wear down the body, but it also causes joy and peace to dissipate. The effects of the atmosphere take a toll on the body, and it cannot remain in its original state. Yes, consequences were designed to kill you.

As sobering as this thought is, it is not the end of the story for those who believe. God is above consequences, and His care and protection of those who believe in Him is evidenced by the fact that though they endure consequences they do not succumb to the consequences. The ability to prevail and produce spiritual fruit in the midst of consequences is the trademark of the faithful. The power of the cross gives us victory over the effects of death. It is one of the many benefits of salvation.

Choosing God's way—a life believing and accepting the work of Jesus Christ—is a choice for salvation and deliverance. God's way produces deliverance not only from sins of the past but also from the sins, trials, tests, and temptations encountered each day. This deliverance is a product of redemption. The resurrection power of Christ takes the sting out of consequences for the believer. Praise God for Jesus!

A powerful Christian life openly displays the benefits of redemption and the power of the resurrection. The fact that the believer not only survives the consequences but prevails with power is miraculous. It shows that power does indeed belong to God. Prevailing with power sends a twofold message: first, that God is all-powerful, and second, that He is at work in the lives of those who believe. Prevailing with power glorifies the name of God and brings you closer to the fulfillment of Romans 12:2: *"And be not conformed to this world: but be ye transformed by the renewing of your mind, that ye may prove what is that good, and acceptable, and perfect, will of God."*

God demonstrates His faithfulness and power to the world by sustaining you through difficult situations. God is faithful and loving. He is unflinchingly committed to His purpose. He will show you that nothing can keep you from achieving what He has in store for you if you will follow Him. Mistakes and misfires can't even derail the purpose of God if you are willing to repent and rely on Him. He makes provision for you and will cause you to prosper. It is truly God's presence with you that makes all the difference. If God is with you who can be against you? Nothing can separate you from the love and power of God (see Romans 8). Consequences that were designed to kill you cannot take you out. God's presence with you gives you the strength, wisdom, and courage to endure the consequences.

Victory over consequences has a remarkable impact on your spiritual walk. When God rescues you from impending death and destruction and you are able to recognize and value it, a greater sense of peace and faith is established in you. You experience the joy of salvation and the certainty of your adoption as a child of God. The knowledge that through

God the power of death from consequences is destroyed sets your life on a course void of anxiety and worry. It positions you for a life of peace and victory. Your confidence in God increases, which leads to greater trust and dependence upon Him. These things are positive outcomes in the life of the believer who recognizes and accepts that forgiveness does not eliminate effects.

While it is important to recognize that consequences are a part of the Christian experience, it is equally important to realize that some things are *not* a part of the experience—namely guilt and shame. Guilt and shame are not tools in the hand of God, even in the administration of consequences. Believers often struggle in their faith walk because guilt, shame, or condemnation causes them to question whether they have been forgiven. There is no need to doubt the work of God. The work of God is established fact. He forgives. God is faithful. His Word is true. If you confess your sin to Him, He forgives you. So then, following true repentance any ensuing guilt that comes is not a work of God.

Condemnation and guilt are enemies to faith. Romans 8:1 helps us to understand that those who are forgiven are no longer condemned, and therefore guilt and shame must depart. *"There is therefore now no condemnation to them which walk not after the flesh, but after the Spirit."* We have been set free from the law of sin and move in accordance with the Spirit. Legally the question is not one centered on forgiveness; it rests on the feelings of guilt. Feeling guilty or responsible does not change the spiritual truth of God's forgiveness. It only weakens your faith and your ability to move forward. This is significant because if you feel guilt or shame, you might reason that the presence of consequences is evidence of you not being forgiven. Ironically, it creates a never-ending cycle of hopelessness. We ask ourselves and others, "If God has forgiven me, why is this still happening in my life?" It becomes easy to revert to truth or consequences type of thinking. Keep in mind that this type of thinking produces a snowball effect. Once it gets moving in your mind it picks up momentum and becomes a powerful force to be reckoned with.

Let me repeat: guilt is not a tool God uses. Overcoming the challenge of guilt and shame can be found in reminding yourself that God has forgiven you. If you continue to hold onto something the Creator of heaven and earth has let go of, then you stand in opposition to Him. Standing on the truth of God's Word erases those feelings. Holding onto feelings of guilt and shame is not a debt you owe. The gift of forgiveness from God took care of all debts. Don't allow those things to dismantle your faith. Don't allow your mind to halt your progress. God forgives you of unrighteousness and propels you into your divine purpose. If consequences cannot kill you, then feelings should not cause you to give up.

Overcoming this is found as you embrace a proper understanding of forgiveness and the role of the Holy Spirit in cleansing and renewing your mind. Doubts about salvation are truly disastrous, that can set off a chain of even greater consequences and situations. Doubt causes faith to erode. And make no mistake about it, your adversary the devil wants your faith to erode. He wants you to believe that God has not forgiven you so that you will live a life of condemnation and unfulfilled purpose. He does not want you to praise God with your life and glorify his name in the earth. He would have you succumb to the negative affects of consequences. Beloved of God you prevail. God's presence and power with you is the best insulation against the effects of consequences. Maintaining a proper attitude is one of the key components of prevailing with power.

Do Not Despise the Consequences

The psalmist wrote that the key to handling consequences is a proper attitude. Experiencing the sometimes-unpleasant effects of our actions can foster poor attitudes. We begin to despise the consequences. We complain about them and what is happening to us. It turns into a pity party. Yet as believers, we must not yield to the temptation to complain or bemoan our circumstances but acknowledge the sovereignty of God in our lives. God is in control of everything, and nothing happens to us that He is not aware of. God does not waste our time or give us busy work to complete while He does something else. If we are enduring consequences then they have a spiritual benefit. Yes, knowledge is critical, but a proper attitude proves to be the best. *"It was good for me that I have been afflicted; that I might learn thy statutes" (Psalm 119:71).*

Consequences, afflictions, and even suffering have a greater work in the life of a believer than temporary discomfort. They work for your good. They work to bring forth truth. God's forgiveness of your sin is factual. To truly reap the benefit of consequences, remember that all things work for your good as long as you love God and are on task to fulfill His purposes. Generally speaking, not many people enjoy affliction, but the pain that comes from it causes you to dig deep to find solutions or relief. That is the sentiment expressed in Psalm 119. Affliction caused the psalmist to look deeper into the Word of God for comfort, understanding, and peace. In the process, he experienced the power of God.

This might seem like a strange thing to say, but the psalmist really provides some powerful insight to help us align our thinking with the will of God. Although the ultimate purpose of consequences is to produce death, when you are in the hand of God you have been given victory over death and sin. God is not a time waster, so instead of producing death the consequences will produce reformation in your life and behavior. Enduring consequences should help you recall the error of your actions and serve as a reminder of what to avoid. This is a powerful reason why we must not despise consequences. The consequences of your actions cannot produce spiritual death as long as you stay under the cover and protection of the Lord. Being able to make the connection between Christ's victory on the cross and the appropriation of that victory in your life is the key to your patience and victory during consequences.

Being a Christian does not make you immune from experiencing the consequences of your actions. And although this seems logical, it is still not easy to accept. In fact, when we are going through difficult times it seems very hard to accept the consequences, and sometimes we even begin to despise them. When we despise the consequences, it is hard to obtain the benefit of them from God's perspective. God's allowing consequences in your life only seeks to reform your thinking and behavior. The experience solidifies your understanding of His will. When things get difficult and it seems like the pressures of the consequences are more than you can bear, remember that God will not put anything on you that you are not capable of handling. You have the power to prevail. You might be tempted to despise the consequences and give up, but it is important to resist the urge to throw in the towel. Do not try to avoid the consequences. Do place your faith and trust in the fact that God is with you. Do believe that God is with you and has a greater plan for your life. Do not be like most, willing and happy to accept forgiveness but despising having to surrender to the work of the Holy Sprit in your life.

No one likes to deal with consequences. However, just as forgiveness does not come without the cleansing from unrighteousness, neither do actions follow without consequences. Believers are unique. Our faith gives us the power to manage life according to kingdom principles and not worldly principles. Abandon the natural human tendency to evade the cleansing and consequences at all costs. Embrace a new and intimate experience with God by allowing your attitude about consequences to be one of gratitude and hope. Experiencing the power of God is not found in escaping the cleansing and consequences. It is in those experiences that we find how real and effectual His workings are. Consequences teach us about God, and what greater gift can we have but to know Him. God will not always allow consequences to disappear. God is not spooky. He is real. His Word is real. He is the same today as He was yesterday and will be tomorrow. If the patriarchs of the Bible had to endure consequences for their actions, we should consider ourselves forewarned and be willing to endure ours.

In fact, having their testimony and witness about enduring consequences teaches us relevant lessons today. By examining the biblical accounts of people who paved the way, our journey of faith is made a little smoother. It is possible to move through our journey without many of the bumps and bruises that come as a result of poor choices. Why, with all the information, is it so difficult to glean from the example of others? One reason could be pure stubbornness. Typically, people feel they need to experience something for themselves to gain a full appreciation of it. Again, this is stubbornness and should be avoided. Stubbornness is as idolatry unto the Lord. Be careful in thinking you must have your own personal experience to believe. Faith says "I believe."

I once worked for an otolaryngologist (ear, nose, and throat doctor) and frequently saw the effects that smoking and chewing tobacco had on people. My observations there further solidified my decision not to smoke. Even if the risks seem minimal it's better to be safe than sorry. Nothing made me want to go out and take a chance on getting the same result. I guess when it comes to negative outcomes I am not much of a risk taker. I just don't need to subject myself to something to see if I could beat the odds. It might be helpful if more people adopted that attitude and stood on the testimony of others instead of taking a risk and trying to beat the odds. Now, there are times when risk taking is warranted, but this is not one of them.

It is the application of the consequences that disciplines you. The Holy Spirit sets out to cleanse you from unrighteousness, and through experiencing painful or challenging consequences an indelible mark is made on your mind. This produces change. It trains you, and discipline occurs. You learn the ways of God. Recall again Psalm 119:71, *"It is good for me that I have been afflicted; that I might learn thy statutes."*

Another thing we must realize is that we are responsible for every choice we make. The good ones, the bad ones, and the ones we make by omission. A lot of times when things don't go well we say, "But I didn't do anything." That could actually be true. Perhaps you didn't do anything and should have. This falls into the category of sins of omission.

Facing the Music

Whatever brings you to the place of enduring consequences, whether personal challenges or the effects of sin in the world, you must be willing to face the music. This point is best illustrated by gleaning another example from the life of David. David was always willing to accept the consequences of his actions. He demonstrates that when we have done wrong, it is important to make the correct choices. Often we try to mitigate the circumstances by covering up or choosing the path of least resistance, yet God desires us to choose Him and the path He ordains regardless of what it contains. We cannot soften the consequences by choosing the easy road. It is not possible to soften the circumstances. God's mercy is the mitigating factor. Spiritual growth is experienced as we select the right path, even if it is not the easy one.

Taking responsibility for your own actions and non-actions is a vital step in your spiritual formation. Too often we are quick to blame others for our shortcomings. Yes it's easier, but it doesn't empower you to make choices and bring change in your life. God always gives us a choice. You may know it as free will, but He always gives us a choice. We make choices every day, some good, some bad, but choices nonetheless. The ability to find the courage to face the music when you've made an incorrect choice develops strength of character and humility in you.

Again we turn to David for a valuable life lesson. The book of Chronicles gives an example of David's census-taking fiasco. In fact, it states that David was provoked by Satan to count the people of Israel. He decided to count the people versus relying on the power and presence of God as he prepared for a battle. Long story short, David lost sight of the fact that Israel had already won several battles because of the Lord's presence with them, and now he felt the need to count the warriors to make a battle plan. He spoke to Joab and the other rulers about his desire, and Joab tried to remind him that it wasn't necessary. Joab knew that with God they could conquer anything. God has power and ability far greater than any number of soldiers. David proceeded to order the census. Bear in mind that no matter what your position, Satan will try to bait you into something. Be very sober and vigilant of this fact. Not every idea you have will be a "God idea." Take the time to reflect on the wisdom and counsel of other godly men and women when they wave a caution flag in front of you.

So David ignored the counsel of those around him and had the men counted. This action caused God to be displeased with him. David's actions set off a series of consequences that resulted in the death of many of his soldiers. The number of men in his army dwindled. These were the same men he was trying to count to ensure he was prepared for the upcoming battle. Wow! David's choice caused the loss of lives. Your choices also carry that much importance. Not only do your choices affect you, but they affect the lives of others. That is a sobering thought; personal actions can result in disastrous consequences for others. It's worth repeating: your actions affect the lives of others. David's decision to take a census resulted in the death of those around him. Our lives are interconnected. No one is so insular that they shouldn't consider others in daily living. The survival of others may be dependent upon the decisions you make. Are you willing to risk it by being selfish or prideful, or will you rely totally on God's guidance and direction to ensure the best possible outcome for everyone?

Making the Right Choice

Another technique used to avoid consequences is passing the buck or blaming other people. Spending time inventing reasons, excuses, and justifications as to why things happened is wasted time. In reality, it is often your response to a situation that needs to be examined. Blaming others may be an attempt to avoid punitive action. You are responsible for the choices you make. The only reason we allow ourselves to do something is because it is already in our heart. We cannot be tempted by that which is not already in our hearts.

> Let no man say when he is tempted, I am being tempted by God; for God cannot be tempted by evil, and He himself does not tempt anyone. But each one is tempted when he is carried away and enticed by his own lust. Then when lust has conceived, it gives birth to sin; and when sin is accomplished, it brings forth death.
>
> James 1:13-15 KJV

You will not be able to avoid the consequences, even if you say "the devil made me do it." Scripture clearly teaches that no man can be tempted except by what is in his own heart.

Avoiding Consequences

David's stubbornness masquerading as the authority of the kingship not only placed him in a tenuous situation, it also affected those around him. He had the counsel of Joab, who provided a gentle reminder of what King David's thoughts and intentions should be, yet he chose to ignore it. He was determined to do what was in his heart. Many times we end up in difficult circumstances because we don't listen to those around us.

There is safety in godly counsel. We cannot allow our own pride, arrogance, or stubbornness to direct our lives. God will use people around us to help us steer clear of trouble, but are we wise enough and humble enough to obey?

Joab reminded King David of the provision and protection of God, and still David went on to do what he wanted. Another lesson we can glean from this encounter between King David and Joab is that subordinates must obey, but their obedience does not guarantee that we are walking in line with God. Joab was required to obey the instruction of the king. This is a word of caution. It is possible to get confused as to whether we are honoring God when people around us obey us. Obedience from a subordinate does not signify accuracy in our decisions. Joab obeyed because he had to, not because the king was right. Consequences helped David realize his error. Everyone who is an authority figure must be cautious of this fact. Regardless of the area of leadership—church, school, home, or work—keep in mind that those who are in a subordinate position to you will obey even if you are wrong. It is important to be skilled in following God. This fact should touch every point of your life, from parenting decisions to those at the office as well as those that pertain to ministry. Be sure you are in line with what God wants and not just what you want, or what is convenient for you.

Whenever you decide to do something that comes out of your own heart and not from the heart of God, you will face consequences that bring you back to the heart of God. David numbered the people with an improper motive. He wanted to know how many people he had to help him win the battle, which shows his reliance was not totally on God. He had confidence in his own ability. Self-reliance is the opposite of humility and detracts from the advancement of God's kingdom. David's action caused Israel to lose people. The account of this event does not say the Lord was displeased with David and so He struck him. Instead, David's error cost Israel seventy thousand men. If God just dealt with us only it would perpetuate our own self-centered thinking, but when others suffer because of our actions it puts everything in a different perspective. God wants us to have a sense of community—common unity. We are all in this together. Someone else's life or salvation might rest on the choices you make. If you are weak in decision making and following after God, perhaps many will suffer the consequences of that weakness.

When the soldiers began to die, David was hurt. He had to face the gravity of his decision. He realized that as a leader he missed the mark and now others paid the price. We see the beauty of David's heart in his recognition of God's displeasure with him. That recognition led to an acknowledgment of sin. David said "I have sinned greatly" and asked for forgiveness. God, in faithfulness, forgave and sent forth consequences to David. Interestingly, David was given an opportunity to make choices concerning his consequences. What an incredible situation to be in. God gives you choices about which road to travel when it comes to consequences. This is not about taking the easy way out; it reveals the nature of your heart. Just as you are responsible for every choice you make, the choices you make are equally revealing. David's choices reveal more of the nature of God as well as the true state of his own heart.

A Look at David's Choices

After the children of Israel experienced the consequences that befell them as a result of David's sin, David began to speak to the Lord. Here again David models the appropriate methods for handling a difficult situation. He did not run from the Lord feeling sorry for himself and ashamed of the mistake he made. He went to God in prayer immediately. David acknowledged his sin and asked for forgiveness. The fact that David often used the word *iniquity* in his confession of sin is important. Iniquity is inward rebellion. It denotes an issue of the heart that leads to deviation from the appointed path of God. Iniquity must be confessed to God, repentance made, and corresponding action taken in response to the forgiveness God grants.

David indeed realized that the consequences facing the children of Israel resulted from his perverse action, the actions of his heart. After his communication with God, God sent him an answer through the seer Gad. Gad presented David three choices of consequences. It might seem strange that God would give David an opportunity to choose his consequences, but God always has a plan that is meant for our good. Each day we are given a choice of life or death, and we of our own free will select the path we wish to follow. God's giving the choices to David allowed the true nature of his heart to be revealed. When we have missed the mark or veered from the path that was originally set before us, God still gives us choices. The choice we make from that point can bring us life or death.

A Closer Look at Our Choices

Through the seer Gad, God gave King David three choices of consequences. He could select either three years of famine, three months of destruction fighting with the enemy, or three days of enduring the sword of the Lord. When David heard the three choices, he realized he was in a serious situation. Each choice was designed to reveal the position of David's heart. Looking at it from a twenty-first-century perspective, the choices we face each day are also designed to reveal to us the workings of our heart. Let's examine the choices David had and how our own choices reveal our true motives and desires.

David sinned because of issues in his heart. The issue could have been that he was not fully trusting in the protection of the Lord. This seems plausible by Joab's response: *"The Lord make his people a hundred times so many more as they be: but, my lord the king, are they not all my lord's servants? Why then doth my lord require this thing? Why will he be the cause of trespass to Israel?" 1 Chronicles 21:3* Even after these words from Joab, David took the census. Once he did, God was angry and issued a choice of consequences. Although consequences are designed to kill you, isn't it incredible that God would actually give you a choice in the matter? God gave David three choices. A tremendous amount of learning can come from these lessons. There is no passing the buck with sin. You will not avoid consequences by blaming someone else for your choices. Satan provoked David, but David made the choice and Israel suffered the consequences.

Practically speaking, we must recognize that the choices we make affect many things. The principle of sowing and reaping applies across the entire spectrum of living, not just in the financial contributions we make. Provocation can only release what was already inside you. Thank God for uncovering darkness, fears, doubts, and insecurities in us to take us to another level of intimacy in Him.

The first choice was three years of famine. Famine speaks of a lack of food. This meant that David and the Israelites would suffer a lack of food and strength for three years. As a result of a famine, strength would diminish, work would diminish, people would die, and others would not be born. A famine would have far-reaching implications that were unable to be calculated at the time. The choice of famine in terms of David's heart issue speaks of a lack of God's provision. If David chose this route, it would demonstrate that somehow he believed he could make his own provision. When you choose famine as a consequence, it demonstrates that you still believe you are able to make your own provision. Perhaps you feel that there will be enough food or you have an abundance of "food" in storage. In choosing famine, you show on some level a lack of submission to God.

How do we choose famine? When we pull away from God because of some sin we have committed, we are leaving or giving up our provision. In essence, we are choosing the consequence of famine when we stop praying, stop attending church, and neglect Bible study and personal devotions because we are ashamed of what we have done or what others might think. Famine speaks to us about the lack of food, but it is important to understand this naturally and spiritually. To be without food is to be without the Word. To be without the Word is to be void of instruction and impartation. Jesus said, "I am the bread that came down from heaven; he who eats and drinks of me shall not thirst or hunger again." Our provision is in God, and when we sin, we must not choose famine for it will only contribute to greater loss and eventually death. David did not choose this.

The second choice was three months of fighting with the enemy—not just three months of fighting but three months of being destroyed. This choice reveals the position of our heart that says we are able to run, fight, and do things in our own strength. We do not fully appreciate the security and protection of the Lord. Somehow, we think we will still be able to outrun or fight the enemy, or even stay just one-step ahead of him, without the Lord. Practically speaking, when we make this choice we will spend a lot of time running, ducking, and dodging yet still being overtaken by our enemies. We may experience intense struggles against us. The war may erupt around our faith, joy, peace, prosperity, and sense of security. We get in a battle over something we are supposed to have anyway by right of ownership and possession, yet the enemy comes to take it away.

During a war nothing is really off limits. There are no areas that your adversary will not touch because they are so special to you. Anything that is considered valuable to you and for you will be on the battleground and open to be destroyed. David didn't make this choice, yet you do when you decide to go into battle without the presence of the Lord. Continuing on your path and thinking you have enough power to prevail, or that the loss won't be that bad, is dangerous. You make this choice when you believe you can overtake the enemy without God's help. It demonstrates that you have placed your sufficiency in yourself and not in God. You are looking at your power. Luke 10:19 says that Jesus gives us the power to prevail against all things. It is not our own strength but God's that is sufficient for every circumstance.

Sometimes it is not easy to know what you have chosen, but you can look at the circumstances of your life to help you see what choices you have made. If you find that the intent to accomplish God's will on your own is prevalent in your life, you may have chosen famine. If you are being attacked on every side, pressed, and perplexed, you may have chosen the period of fighting and fleeing and not the path of submission. God gives us provision daily as we look to Him and submit to His leading. David did not choose this.

The final choice was three days of being under the sword and pestilence of the Lord. Three days is significantly shorter than three years and about eighty-seven days shorter than three months of consequences, yet there is a huge unknown variable here. What will God actually do? It is impossible for man to calculate what the Lord will do to us. So the question becomes am I willing to trust Him? This choice reveals a heart attitude of trust and commitment to the Lord. Even though the time is shorter, we are often inclined to run from God instead of run to Him. We fear that He will make life unusually hard for us. We reason that the punishment might be too hard to bear, but this choice helps us to realize that if our heart is centered on the Lord and pleasing Him, then we are willing to put all our trust in Him. We do not run away from Him but run toward Him. We believe just as Job did that "though He slay me, yet will I trust Him." With these three choices, David realized he was in a big mess and decided to fall into the hands of the Lord, knowing that God possesses greater mercy than man. David chose this one. He decided to make the choice for God's way. He demonstrated that God can be trusted. God's strength and ability to provide for us is better than counting on the mercies of our enemy and the unknown implications of famine. God is faithful and merciful.

David's choice did indeed reveal the true nature of his heart. He was totally dependent upon the Lord. He trusted that God alone would make provision for him, provide protection, and mete out justice. David essentially said, "It is better to take my chances with my God, the one I have experience with, the one who knows me, than rely on myself." You too must realize that in choosing your consequences your chances of survival, overcoming, and subsequent victory are all tied to your willingness to choose God. Consequences are designed to kill you; however, if you totally rely upon God He will ensure that you ultimately prevail. Even if you get hurt a little during the journey, you will prevail!

Recall from the experience of David that life is not just about you and your way. It is about many others. Your life connects to the lives of others. Your choices affect others in more powerful ways than you think. David took a census and God smote Israel, leading to the death of seventy thousand men. David's subsequent confession, repentance, and choosing the proper consequence led to restoration, but only after tremendous suffering and loss. All in all, he was forgiven and went on to do great things in the name of the Lord, but you too must appreciate the far-reaching implications of your actions. Although the adversary would like nothing more than your death from the consequences, God wants you to learn of Him and refine your decision- making processes to be in line with the principles of His kingdom.

Ultimately, choosing the consequence administered by God will preserve your life and produce fruitfulness in you. When you have chosen the God path, your experience should reflect increases in your personal walk in the following areas:

- Humility
- Compassion
- Faith
- Obedience
- Trust

On your journey, remember the choice is yours. You can choose to believe that you will not receive consequences for your actions or recognize that consequences will come. The fruit of your choices affect more than you alone. Your ability to make the proper choice is really governed by the true condition of your heart. You can believe that God will rescue you from all your consequences, or you can understand that in the hands of God consequences can become His instrument to work righteousness into you. The fact remains that men and women make mistakes and consequences happen, yet one struggles, withers, and dies while the other endures hardship, gains strength, and prevails. The difference is God. When God is with you who can be against you? For God indeed has defeated death. I challenge you today to make the God choice at all times for in it lies your salvation and your increase. God did not say there would be no consequences, but with God, you prevail with power!

Renew Your Mind...

Think about the previous chapter. What challenged your thinking in this area? Take a moment and interact with the material by journaling your perspective prior to reading and your thoughts now. Note any shift in paradigms.

_____
_____
_____
_____
_____
_____
_____

Transform Your Walk...

Change occurs when we move from thinking to doing. Change involves action. What consequences have you encountered in your life that left you questioning whether God was with you or not? Do you need to evaluate the choices you are making concerning your consequences? Are you choosing famine, foes, or falling into the hands of God? You can change your perspective during this time by making the God choice. List some consequences and think about how you can now begin to see that God is with you.

_____
_____
_____
_____
_____
_____
_____
_____

Chapter Three

God Didn't Say...
Obedience Is Optional

~~~

"And Samuel said, Hath the Lord as great delight in burnt offerings and sacrifices, as in obeying the voice of the Lord? Behold, to obey is better than sacrifice, and to hearken than the fat of rams." 1 Samuel 15:22

Setting the Stage

Johnny was a kid out of control. He demanded things from his mother and deliberately ignored her attempts to reason with him. His mother slowly moved up the aisle of the super-market embroiled in what seemed to be a battle of wills. She spoke to him in a calm, sweet voice as if she didn't want to anger him by being firm. That was aisle two. As I left the aisle, he apparently had not gotten his way because I heard him begin to scream and whine. Of course, as a mother of four children, I had a lot of thoughts about what could and should happen, but I simply prayed for them and continued on with my shopping. A few minutes later I met up with Johnny and his mother again in the checkout line. As we waited for our respective turns to pay for our groceries, Johnny plunged into another episode. His mother, looking a little tired and frustrated with him, said, "Johnny, you cannot have candy, we are going to have lunch in a few minutes. You want pizza don't you?" Then the reply, "I don't want pizza; I want M&Ms." Mom continued, "Well, you can't have M&Ms now, maybe later. Johnny, please come over here and stand next to me." "I don't want to stand next to you; I want M&Ms." "Johnny, come over here and stand next to me." He froze, holding a pack of M&Ms, and started to open the pack of candy. His mother said, "You can come over here like I said, or you can just stand there in the way of the other people. What would you like to do? Obey me or disobey?"

Though this episode could be a book all by itself, it provided a clear example of how we respond to the request for obedience. As I watched this episode, a million fire alarms were ringing in my head. I thought, *When did obedience become optional?* Then it hit me: this was exactly the type of behavior that contributes to the belief that obedience is optional. When it comes to spiritual growth, the belief that obedience is optional is an erroneous thought indeed. Obedience is not optional. It is required. Yes, the decision to obey or disobey is within our power, but really it is no choice at all because disobedience brings consequences and the consequences for disobedience are designed to kill you.

Sometimes when the consequences of our disobedience seem miniscule or even nonexistent, we are led to think obedience does not matter. Obedience matters. God commanded obedience from the beginning. He even said that it is better than sacrifice.

Obedience demonstrates many things: trust, respect for authority, and reverence for God. Through obedience, we show our true trust in Him. Disobedience is so prevalent in our lives and society because the repercussions are not always immediately visible. The problem with living only by that which is seen is that it stands in direct contradiction to a life of faith. Remember that we walk by faith and not by sight. So does that mean we should disobey just because there is a chance we won't get caught? No. The power of Christianity is found in the ability to obey. As believers we understand that what we do or don't do has eternal consequences. Again, for the record, obedience is not an optional element of Christianity. It cannot be turned on and off according to feelings or circumstances.

Obedience is a major component of a powerful spiritual walk. The principles and practice of obedience should be clearly understood by every man or woman who wants to deepen their relationship with God. Throughout history, every man or woman who has gained favor with God and man has been a student of the divine school of obedience. Obedience is at the core of experiencing and accessing the true power of God. Obedience reveals the glory of God. Obedience provides the power to change lives and advance the kingdom of God. Obedience causes you to be protected in all situations. If obedience releases the glory of God, causes you to triumph in situations, and is at the core of experiencing and accessing the true power of God, why is it such a challenge to spiritual growth? From a spiritual standpoint, too much of the world's thinking clutters the minds of many believers. It is necessary to dismiss the popular notions about obedience and embrace the truth and power of God's Word. By allowing your mind to be renewed to the truth of obedience, you can make a stronger connection to God. God is waiting on you to make that connection. Our experience with obedience is also challenged by poor habits. The habit of compromising instead of obeying what God says leads to a life with insufficient power to expand the kingdom. In order to move into victory, glory, and power the mind must be renovated. This occurs as we dismantle spiritual myths and replace them with biblical truth.

Addressing Spiritual Myths

Many of the biggest delusions of our time happen in this area. Believers frequently think that our situations are unique and therefore require some other remedy than adherence to the word of God. Yet, the word of God is the solution for all that we experience. It heals us, mind, body, soul, spirit. It heals our thinking, our speaking, and our actions. The righteousness of God is found in the word. When we obey the word we are alive in Christ and he is alive in us.

In the Garden of Eden, the serpent tricked Eve by simply planting seeds of doubt. Doubt causes a lack of clarity. It produces a gray area. Yet God's plan does not contain any gray areas. Any perceived gray area would be considered middle of the road. The middle of the road is the place of being lukewarm and God would have no part of that. Interpretation of our own accord is not profitable and sometimes dangerous.

Sometimes our thoughts surrounding obedience are too vague. As children we learn that obedience is doing exactly what you are told. We experience consequences for not doing something or for doing the wrong thing. Understanding the principle seems quite easy here—obey and stay out of trouble. As we grow we find the introduction of "gray" because as we see it people don't obey everything and still seem to fare quite well. This thought stays with us as we move into adulthood. We find that our views on obedience have become ambiguous. No longer does obedience in our lives rest solely on the basis that following instruction is good but it begins to blur. We try to add factors in our decision making like who will know, what will happen if I don't or even thoughts like nobody else seems to receive any punishment for this. These thoughts simply confuse the matter of obedience. It causes an impure definition to become the basis of how we obey. A lack of clarity about the power of obedience causes a "Saul-like" mentality to be developed when it comes to following instructions. The "Saul-like mentality" says, "I will obey with the interjection of my own thoughts."

Our thoughts on obedience must be explored. Obedience is not accomplished in degrees. Saul, the first king of Israel, thought that almost being obedient was good enough. He almost did what God said, except that he kept the best sheep and spared the life of the enemy king. His partial obedience cost him the entire kingdom. As with Saul, the notion that obedience is optional is reflected in the tapestry of our lives through a variety of ways. First, consider the example with little Johnny at the beginning of the chapter. When we are given the choice to obey or disobey we tend to build a house around that framework. Another contributing factor is that we redefine what it means to be obedient to suit our needs. Somehow we believe our situation is different or special, and therefore God will understand our inability to obey and give us a pass on obeying His Word.

The command to obey was given at the very beginning of time. Yet, in the Garden of Eden the seeds of disobedience were sown. Those seeds still cause problems in our lives today by affecting our thinking and behavior. But we are able to uproot the seeds that lead to destruction and cultivate the seeds of obedience that bring us blessing, favor, and peace. Your experience of life victorious begins when you face erroneous thoughts about obedience, begin to see it from God's perspective, and walk in the power that He has placed in you. Today, you can begin to destroy the seeds of disobedience and embrace the truth and power that comes from obeying God with your whole heart. It begins with taking a look at some of the myths surrounding obedience.

Myth 1: I am the exception to the rule (aka my situation is unique)

One of the biggest delusions of all is that our unique situation bears some special significance that warrants an exception to God's principles. God's principles do not possess exceptions. When the Word says love thy neighbor as thyself, it does not mean if thy neighbor is nice to you and you get along fine. When the Word tells us to forgive, it does not make an exception to the rule because the offense is especially heinous. It simply tells us to forgive. The principles of God are sure and firm. Thinking your situation is somehow outside the scope of the Word only leads to rationalization and justification of your actions. There is no justification for missing the mark. If God says "do it" then just do it. Living an obedient life will open the door to levels of wisdom, power, and strength you have never imagined. A narrow definition of obedience to fit your life will never produce God's power and results in your life.

Myth 2: I did almost everything God said

This is a false premise. Partial obedience is still disobedience. My Latin teacher used to say, "Almost is never near enough except in horseshoes and atomic bombs"—meaning that almost is only accepted as a part of those two situations. He was a man of wisdom. Doing almost everything God said cost Saul the kingdom and a blessed lineage. When it comes to the instructions of the Lord, partial obedience is still disobedience. It goes on record in heaven as rebellion.

Think about it. God's instructions to Saul were clearly outlined by the prophet Samuel. He was to destroy the Amalekites—lock, stock and barrel. Yet, Saul did not do what was required. He managed to save the best of the sheep, rams, gold, and the king. He even tried to explain his deviant behavior by claiming to have done it for God. His excuse was that he wanted to sacrifice to God and knew that God wanted the best. Funny, how Saul confronted by Samuel and found in the midst of disobedience lies and refuses to take responsibility for his actions. He even tries to through God in the mix by claiming he held the best to sacrifice unto the Lord.

Saul's own pride and selfish desires kept him locked in the chains of disobedience. His thinking that he could somehow do it his way and still please God cost him the kingdom.

Unfortunately many of our attitudes and thoughts about obedience are the same as Saul's. Making excuses, shifting responsibility, throwing in the occasional, "I did this to honor God" all seem to sometimes be par for the course. None of these things negate the effect of a lack of obedience. Disobedience places you the same position as Saul— losing.

Ironically, this example wasn't the first time Saul disobeyed God but it was the one that yields us the powerful words, "to obey is better than to sacrifice" and helps clarify the fact that there is a limit to the life expectancy of disobedience. Though the concept of obedience can seem vague, the perfect life of Jesus teaches us something valuable about obedience. It is never simply a surface issue.

Myth 3: I will obey as soon as I can

Delayed obedience is disobedience and dishonors God. When instructions are given and not followed, there is a reason. Although the individual excuses may vary, usually the reason is that the person is still deciding whether to obey. Most of the time delayed obedience is rooted in what a person believes is right, not whether they want to do what is right. To delay means that something has taken priority over fulfilling the instructions given. If your delay is based on the fact that you have something to do first, you have missed the mark. Sometimes we hide delayed obedience behind the wall of prayer. We feel a particular leading to do something but when asked to step forward we refuse which causes us to delay. Delayed obedience is disobedience. It is important to acknowledge that fact. Many times, we fall into this sin through the subtle deception of our minds. Think about it, when someone asks you to do something and you want to you give an immediate answer and get on with the task at hand; yet when something comes up that you don't want to do or have some reservations about there is a necessity to pray about it and get back with the person. Now, I know there are a variety of situations and circumstances that can be applied but just for a moment think about it in your religious setting. Your pastor or care group leader comes to you and asks you to do something. You are uncertain or perhaps don't even want to do it. So you say, "I'll pray about it and get back with you." Instead of it truly being an issue of prayer is a method of avoidance. It is important to move beyond this type of avoidance in order to possess greater spiritual power.

Delayed obedience is often the result of unbelief. Our thoughts about the optional nature of obedience are revealed daily. Unfortunately, the decision to obey is many times based on how we feel about a situation and not the requirement. When we feel good about something and it meets our criteria for passing the standard, we think, *Okay, I'll do it, but only when it fits into my schedule.*

God requires radical obedience. The believer concerned with spiritual growth cannot afford to fall into the "I'll do it later" trap. Being sensitive to the will and timing of the Lord is important for spiritual growth. God's timing is perfect. Ecclesiastes declares that there is a time to sow, a time to reap, a time to work, and a time to rest, etc. Things move in accordance with the divine timeline of the Lord. Our obedience is tied to God's timeline. Delay moves you beyond a defined measure of time. Whenever delay occurs, the action that should have taken place at a specific time doesn't happen, causing a series of events that didn't have to be a part of your experience. If we neglect the importance of timing, we stand to live a life of missed opportunities. Missed timing and failed opportunities cannot be regained. It is important to understand the correlation between obedience and timing. If you again consider the fact that God has a bigger plan, your timely obedience stands as a point of protection. It protects you because as you complete the tasks that are required, you ensure that you are doing the proper work in the proper season. Your obedience can be the foundation of preparation for something to come. If you disobey, time continues to move forward and you might find that you are not equipped to handle the situation. Obedience is not optional.

Myth 4: The people made me do it

"The people made me do it," or better yet, "the devil made me do it" are excuses that are often given in response to disobedience because we think if we can hold another person accountable it somehow makes the situation better. Disobedience cannot be blamed on any other person. You have choices in everything. The fact of the matter is that people (and even the devil) cannot make you do anything that is not already desired in your heart. If you have a heart to disobey then you will. If you have a heart to obey then you will. Circumstances do not make you who you are; your true character is revealed in the circumstance. 1 Samuel 15 tells the story of Israel's first king and the disobedience that caused him to lose everything. In the biblical account, the prophet Samuel told Saul that the Lord wanted him to destroy all the things of the Amalekite kingdom. He specifically instructed him to destroy everything. King Saul did not obey. After Saul disobeyed, he told Samuel that he had reserved the best sheep and the Amalekite king to make an offering unto the Lord. He told him the people wanted to do it. It sounds incredibly similar to Aaron's defense to Moses when they built and worshipped the golden calf. Aaron, in essence, said the people made me do it. Saul, in his disobedience claimed the same thing. It did not work for Aaron, it did not work for Saul and it does not work for us. When it comes to obeying God, you must stand boldly on the Word and not be persuaded by the thoughts and ideas of others. Thinking that if you can blame another it will lessen the consequences for you is really not in line with the Scriptures. The 18th chapter of Ezekiel makes it clear that every man is responsible for his own actions. No one can blame another. You always have a choice.

Myth 5: I can cover my disobedience with a sacrificial offering

God does not look for sacrifices just for the sake of having a sacrifice. When sacrifice is offered to cover up disobedience, it is not acceptable. Again, think of Saul. He disobeyed the instructions of the Lord and tried to cover it up by offering God a sacrifice. God looks on the heart and not the outward appearance. It is similar to disobeying the commandment to love your neighbor as yourself, yet you fast and pray to get closer to God. Sacrifice for the sake of sacrifice is not accepted by the Lord. Believers must move away from empty practices and live their lives in alignment with the will of God.

As a concept, obedience doesn't receive much attention beyond the parenting arena. This is not a problem for our understanding since God is our Father. In the parenting relationship, a child must obey their parents. The parents know what is right, good, and proper for the child. They convey this to the child through instruction. When the child obeys, life is good. There is peace, joy, tranquility, and sometimes even reward. When the child disobeys there is sadness, pain, chaos, and penalty. The child learns to obey through the experiences he endures. Now, on a higher level, as children of God we are told that there are blessings for obedience and curses for disobedience. God wants us to choose peace, joy, and tranquility. The relevance to a powerful Christian walk should not be underestimated. Obedience will produce a life without compromise. It will produce a life of power. It will produce a life where consistency in thought and action reign supreme. Obedience releases the glory of God. It plows the pathway for the Lord of glory to come. It sets you apart as a man or woman who can be trusted by God. Most importantly, it is required by God.

Obedience to God allows the influence of your work to be greater than you could imagine. God's focus is how the power of obedience affects the creation. Hebrews 5:8 says, *"Though he were a son, yet learned he obedience by the things which he suffered."* This scripture is pivotal to properly understanding the weightiness of obedience. Jesus learned obedience by the things He suffered. The word *learned* means to bring into experience or to understand; to know with a moral bearing and responsibility. Essentially, this tells us that Jesus was able to bring the power attached to obedience into experience. He was an example for us to follow. The outward manifestation of the power of God is securely wrapped up in the lesson of obedience. Through His willing subjection to the Father He was able to heal the sick, cast out demons, and cure all manner of sickness and disease.

Our obedience can have the same effect. Demonstrating the power of God on earth and expanding the kingdom should be our motivating factors. The key is that Jesus was able to demonstrate to us the power of obedience. Our willing subjection to the will of God expands His authority on earth. Obedience releases power. Obedience overcomes a perceived lack of authority, equipping, gifting, skill, or talent because it connects you to the Father's authority and power. The fear of being ill-equipped, unskilled, or not talented enough to accomplish something is a smoke screen the adversary uses to hinder the forward progression of believers. In order to overcome those issues, remember that greater is He that is in you than he that is in the world. Your obedience partners you with the strength, wisdom, and power of heaven. If the adversary can keep you concerned about your lack as opposed to focused on the ability of God, he has found a way to thwart the expansion of God's kingdom.

Understand the principle here. You must operate in obedience to release the power of God into a situation. If you are fearful and do not walk in alignment with the Word of God, the power of that Word can never be released. God does not circumvent man's faith, trust, or belief to cause something to happen, not even something He desires. Man must willingly submit and obey God. God has given man authority on earth that should reflect His authority and operation in heaven. God will not violate what He has given. Since obedience opens the flow of God's power into situations, it stands to reason that this concept would be a major source of spiritual conflict. Through our obedience the world sees that God indeed exists and has all power. The release of God's glory and power leaves man without excuse when it comes to acknowledging the work of Jesus Christ. Disobedience puts mankind in a position to deny God, deny His power, and reject salvation. Disobedience opens the door to a loss of privilege and power, and possibly brings about deadly consequences. The catastrophic effects of disobedience can not only affect you but others. Even small acts of disobedience may cause you to relinquish the blessings purposed for your life.

Saul, the first king of Israel, disobeyed God and lost the rule of the kingdom. He lost the eternal blessing upon his life and the lives of those who would come after him. He also lost the presence of the Lord. We too, in the face of disobedience, stand to lose our peace, power, and privilege. Is that much loss worth sacrificing your God-ordained purpose? Instead of being willing to sacrifice our peace, power, and privilege we should seek to maximize it all by taking a stand to obey. A life submitted to the Word of God provides divine protection and gives incomparable access to divine power. Choosing to obey is an act of worship. You are accepting God's will above your own. You are putting Him first. Obedience is the most powerful demonstration of your worship towards God and it comes with great blessing and benefit.

In the battle to reveal the glory of God, man must be free from deception. Although there are many myths and delusions surrounding obedience, to have a powerful, Christ-centered spiritual life those myths must be dismantled and truth received.

Life situations sometimes seem confusing and cause us to wonder if complete obedience matters. This confusion sometimes causes the tendencies of compromise to develop. Compromise affects power. The truth is obedience inherently carries an element of power that cannot be understood or experienced when compromised is present. If you are realizing the full power of obedience in your life, accept that obedience is not optional. Declare not only in word but also in deed that obedience is better than sacrifice. Your ability to realize the hidden power of obedience is in your hands.

Your Obedience and God's Plan

Everyone has a plan and purpose for his or her life, one that was ordained by God. With a plan and purpose come gifts, skills, and talents. Many people discover their purpose and work tirelessly using their gifts, skills, and talents to accomplish their dreams and desires. Ironically, using your gifts, skills, and talents is the not the key to the perfect life. The ability to use those gifts, skills, and talents in obedience with the will of God propels you into abundant living. Of course, not using your gifts, skills, and talents the way God intended is considered rebellion. But to use them according to your own will or desire can be just as detrimental when it comes to overall life satisfaction. Each one of us was created to powerfully connect to our Creator and to release His glory in the earth. When you live your life in accordance with the will of God, you bring glory and honor to Him and you gain eternal reward.

Consider this point. In society, some people are supposed to be teachers. At some point in their life they recognized it, they honored it by getting equipped, and ultimately they became teachers. They love teaching. They know they are supposed to do it. After a time of teaching they begin to feel unfulfilled and dissatisfied. They have not experienced the complete satisfaction, power, and authority that come from fulfilling individual purpose in conjunction with God's divine purpose. When they step into the classroom void of the love, knowledge, and wisdom of God, they can only offer what the world has given them to use. The motivation of a believer should be different from that of the unbeliever. Using the things of the world does not equate to the power and dominion that come from using the principles of God.

When a person feels unfulfilled they seek change. Ironically, the change isn't always about a second or new career; sometimes the change is directly related to firming up their relationship with God. Although many have made the fulfillment of purpose about a task or job, it is more than that, it is ultimately about relationship. God's love for us is not based on our job, title, or talent. His love for one who is a doctor is the same as the one who is a stay at home mom and is the same as the one who teaches kindergarten. God measures our success not on what we do but our heart as we do it. If our hearts are tender to His touch, and our ears attentive to His voice then regardless of our vocation we are reveal His glory and power through our lives. It is through our obedience to Him that we really prove that God's will is good, perfect, and acceptable. Therefore, when you pursue change do it in the light of God's will in obedience to His Word and you will experience life in an amazing way. Obedience is the bridge that connects you and the purpose of God, which causes you to experience true fulfillment.

Imparting the Facts

Obedience is one of the most important aspects of your spiritual walk because it opens up the door to divine power. This power is not just about acquiring personal success; a life of power can be used in the service of others and have greater kingdom effect. You can have gifts, talents, skills, passion, and desire, but partnering with God increases their effectiveness. An obedient man or woman in the hand of God is far more valuable than a man or woman of many gifts, skills, and talents who does not rely on God. Why? Because God possesses all power, authority, and skill. The Holy Spirit is able to endow you with power, skill, or ability in a circumstance that will cause you to prevail. When a person is obedient, God equips them to do a multitude of things. A person with many skills, gifts, and talents can do many things, but the absolute perfection comes with doing those things in obedience to God. Doing this is only possible when you acknowledge that there is a bigger picture than your personal gain. This is the mind of the kingdom expander. Obedience is the mind of Christ. An obedient man or woman has embraced the vision God established for the earth and knows that through their obedience they are helping things come to pass. Obedience is required.

Obedience is the result of revelation and belief. The worshipper of God obeys God. Not only does the worshipper of God obey God, but they also obey God's delegated authority. For not to obey would really mean there is no revelation of God.

A New View of Obedience

When we consider the ramifications of obedience we must face the fact that delayed obedience is really disobedience in disguise. Though we can come up with a million reasons why we were not prompt, the root of delayed obedience is rebellion. This may strike a very serious chord with some because we tend to think our reasons, justifications, and excuses are acceptable, but they are not. For example, let's say you are the parent of a teenager and give them the task of cleaning the kitchen. Suddenly the phone rings. The teenager stops to talk on the phone instead of completing the task, thinking, *I'll just get to it later.* When you come back to the kitchen and see that it's not finished, yet your teenager is on the phone, you are not interested in what caused the delay. You only care that they did not follow your instructions. Likewise, when we are told to do something for God and we have very good reasons for delaying such as "the phone rang," or "I got caught in traffic," or even "I wanted to pray one more time," God is not interested in what caused the delay. His primary concern is that you did not complete the task you were given to do.

The Root of Delay

The challenge most believers have is that they believe they can hear God and that His instructions are always superbly in line with their thoughts, personality, and desires. We have developed a society where we think God is on our level. God is not on our level. We can't figure Him out, nor can we get comfortable.

I remember a particular call to do something radical for God. I thought, *That doesn't make sense to me, the devil is a liar, I am not doing it.* But then I heard the Holy Spirit say, *Yes, he is, and I told you to do it.* I did it and without anymore delay. Most times, we have no trouble obeying if it seems right to us, but God never said that all His instructions would seem right or good to you. He simply said that when we obey we would be blessed. It is important to keep in mind that God's thoughts are not our thoughts. His ways are much higher than ours are. He sees the bigger picture and our view is limited.

Think of Abraham for a moment. God didn't tell him something that seemed okay to him. Yet he determined to obey God no matter what. His only thought was *I will obey.* In fact, it seemed as if his obedience would lie in direct opposition to what God had promised. He was to sacrifice Isaac, the one through whom the promise would come. It was the laying down of his hopes and dreams, the end of an era, so to speak, but Abraham had enough trust in God to say, *Well, at least if I take him up and sacrifice him then God must be up to something.* I believe that Abraham, because of his experience with God, had a divine revelation of the resurrection and the life. We must stand as Abraham did and realize that whenever God tells us to do something, He has a plan that is bigger and better than anything we could ever imagine.

Something about obedience struck me one day as I read the story of the call of Gideon in Judges. Gideon was having a conversation with an angel of the Lord, who told him some incredulous things. "Gideon, you are a mighty man of valor. Gideon, you are going to save Israel. Gideon, I am with you." Things too marvelous for Gideon to believe. So when it came down to it, Gideon asked for confirmation. He didn't ask for confirmation on what he was told was going to happen, nor on what he had to do, but he asked for confirmation on who was talking to him. I believe this is at the heart of all obedience. When you know that you have been communicating with the Lord, you simply obey. He is the Lord of the earth. He created everything.

As the wife of a Solider, I am familiar with the concept of receiving and obeying orders. It is a huge part of our lives. Yet, I often wonder why obedience seems like such foreign concept in other areas of life, especially the church. One day I asked the Lord that question, and His response was somewhat amazing. He told me the military model is good. It represents how things should be in the kingdom. Yet, the Kingdom system is a little more advanced. Submission and obedience in the kingdom are not merely outward displays but the reality of revealed truth. Obedience has just as much to do with the heart as it does with the outward action. If you have enough power, authority, or influence, you will get people to listen to you. In the military enough rank actually gets people to obey you, but they do it outwardly only. Outward obedience is obedience without honor. Obedience without honor does not bring the spiritual effects that make a powerful Christian life.

Practically speaking, we are often faced with life situations that cause us to obey outwardly God but inwardly there is no connection to the power of the Spirit. We are trying to reap a spiritual harvest but only sowing corruption. Take for example the woman whose husband begins to talk of wanting a divorce. She knows intellectually that she should continue to love him and honor the relationship but she is angry, hurt, and confused. She goes about daily life doing the things she is "supposed" to do but not motivated by love. This causes even more problems and challenges in the relationship. In this instance, she obeyed God but that obedience came out of fear, not out of true love. Our obedience must be propelled by love not because we are afraid of what will come if we do not obey. Fear of the Lord is not meant to be understood as being petrified of His coming or His presence. We must learn to honor God through our obedience.

> Though he were a Son, yet learned he obedience by the things which he suffered; and being made perfect, he became the author of eternal salvation unto all them that obey him.
>
> Hebrews 5:8-9

Obedience demonstrates relationship—the type, tone, and tenor of the relationship. Somehow we have come to a place where we believe that when we want to do something and ask God for instructions, then we get those instructions and follow them, we have been obedient. This is too narrowly construed. Obedience is not declared because of one act but because of consistency on a holistic level.

Moving Into Power—Applying It to Your Life

The best way to grow in obedience is to embrace the following spiritual truths about the concept. If you will embrace these truths and position yourself to renew your mind, you will establish a new pattern in your life.

- Truth #1: Delayed obedience is disobedience
- Truth #2: Partial obedience is disobedience
- Truth #3: You are responsible for your own actions
- Truth #4: Obedience is better than sacrifice

Have this attitude in yourselves which was also in Christ Jesus, who although he existed in the form of God did not regard equality with God a thing to be grasped, but emptied Himself taking the form of a bond servant, and being made in the likeness of men. And being found in appearance as a man, he humbled himself by becoming obedient to the point of death, even death on the cross.

Philippians 2:5-8 KJV

There are aspects of surrendering to God that we don't even begin to investigate. We just say the right things. We have become a people skilled at saying the right things; however, the evidence of whether we are in true alignment with the mind of Christ is seen in our daily experiences. Our alignment with Christ is seen in our marriages, in our parenting, on our jobs, in the church, in our friendships, in our adversarial relationships, in our private time alone. Everything we do, say, and think is evidence of our alignment or misalignment with God on the issue.

Let me make it a little clearer. If I am rebellious against my parents, then I prove that I am rebellious against God. If I am prideful and arrogant at work, then it proves that I am prideful and arrogant before God. If I am driven and ruled by my emotions, then it proves that I am driven and ruled by my emotions in things pertaining to God. Even more clarity: If you will lie and cheat at a board game, then why is it such a great leap to believe you will not do the same thing in life? A board game has little consequence in the grand scheme of things; therefore it is easy to infer that when life, which holds much more significance, presents a challenge you will respond accordingly. Let me say it again another way: if you have a child who will defy your rules and regulations, why do you find it hard to believe they will do it in another location? Or that they won't do worse than that?

See, we choose to live each day defending what we want to defend, and sometimes we allow things to cloud our judgment when in fact we have become a hindrance to God. When the disciples told Jesus "Your mother and brother are outside," He responded, "Who is My mother and who is My brother—those who do the will of My Father." Jesus respected and loved His family, but He made it clear that if you were not doing the will of God, you were no relation to Him. We must take the same mind.

I can recall, growing up, that my mother placed a high premium on the truth. The truth was absolutely required. It was so required that if you told an untruth (a lie), you would receive thirty days' restriction for the lie and then the punishment for whatever you did, so if you lied the minimum time served was thirty days. What she taught me was to tell the truth. Her logic behind it was more important than the days or the consequences. She later explained to me, "If you tell me the truth and I can trust your word, I will defend you like no other, but if you lie to me, the one who is responsible for you, then I will deliver you to the enemy." She didn't know it then, but she taught me a principle of God, and that is to always honor the truth.

At the heart of obedience is total surrender to God. This involves walking openly and obediently before Him. It involves surrendering your will to His. It demands that you have complete allegiance to him and have no element of fraud in you. Obedience is not an optional element of Christianity. It cannot be turned on and off according to our feelings or circumstances. If God says "do it" then just do it. Living an obedient life will open the door to levels of wisdom, power, and strength you have never imagined.

Renew Your Mind...

Think about the previous chapter. What challenged your thinking in this area? Take a moment and interact with the material by journaling your thoughts prior to reading and your thoughts now.

_____
_____
_____
_____
_____
_____
_____
_____
_____
_____

Transform Your Walk...

Change occurs when we move from thinking to doing. Change involves action. What steps to being obedient can you take today that will strengthen your spiritual walk?

_____
_____
_____
_____
_____
_____
_____
_____
_____
_____
_____

Chapter Four

God Didn't Say...
Performance Equals Purpose

"Not every one that saith unto me, Lord, Lord, shall enter into the kingdom of heaven; but he that doeth the will of my Father which is in heaven." Matthew 7:21

Setting the Stage

It is no surprise that the world's definition of success is different from God's. Typically success is measured in terms of financial gain, prestige, or popularity, but God doesn't view success the same way. He doesn't have a problem with money, wealth, or other forms of prosperity. It's just that His view of success is more holistic than the popular way of thinking. Each year a very prominent magazine releases several lists of the richest or most successful people. Their lists range from ranking the richest people in the world to the most affluent or highest paid actors and actresses. Anyone looking at the lists would conclude that you are successful when your bank account reveals high dollar amounts. Yet that is not the ideal measure of success. Financial prosperity is only one aspect of success, and even that can truly be subjective. Perhaps financial fitness is a better phrase to use with regard to success. Many people in the world are extremely successful but will never have millions of dollars. They have financial freedom. Their most prized possession is a life of fulfillment.

Believers must recognize that performance does not necessarily equal fulfillment of purpose or success in the eyes of God. Subscribing to the popular standard of success can cause you to lose out on the most important measure of success in the world—a thriving and true relationship with God. A careful reading of Matthew 7:21-23 provides more information about this concept. Let's take a look.

> "Not everyone that saith unto me, Lord, Lord, shall enter into the kingdom of heaven; but he that doeth the will of my Father which is in heaven. Many will say to me in that day, Lord, Lord, have we not prophesied in thy name? and in thy name have cast out devils? and in thy name done many wonderful works? And then I will profess unto them, I never knew you: depart from me, ye that work iniquity.

The workers in the account above had obviously performed great deeds, but their performance did not fulfill the purpose of their lives and they were denied access to the Father.

We must not become so enthralled with the world's definition of success that we start to sacrifice our God-given identity to achieve things with no eternal value. It might be easy to become captivated by the allure of the dollar, but this is not the reason you were created. Your purpose is bigger than things. Fulfilling your purpose is even bigger than creating a name for yourself. We often feel that our achievements tell the world who we are, but consider this radical statement: you were not created to tell the world who you are but to tell the world in word and deed who God is. Our achievements and the drive to pursue our purpose, destiny, and dreams should all originate from the throne room. It is important to keep a constant check on motivations and agendas.

Somehow things got a little twisted and we began to believe that performance equals purpose and fame equals success. We pursue purpose because we want to do something. We want to be respected or considered special. Our desire to obtain things or satisfy a longing can cause us to get so consumed with performance that we actually lose sight of God's original plan. The complete fulfillment of your purpose hinges on the strength of you being who God says you are. When you are being your authentic self, *doing* becomes natural and easy. Being your authentic self, according to God's description of you, produces peace, joy, and fulfillment that is incomparable to anything else you can imagine.

The struggle with accomplishing our purpose is not because we lack intellect, skill, gifts, or talents but often because of our refusal to "be." We are created beings. The word *being* itself brings perspective that all we do should arise out of who we are. This is the way of God. Everything God created came out of who He is. It is good and perfect and shall not be conquered. Subsequently, our fulfillment of purpose develops out of who we are. It is directly in line with God's will. But we must remember that our salvation is not in the *doing* it is in the *being*. Salvation is a work of the heart, and fulfilling purpose is a work that is directly in line with God's will.

God has already spoken a powerful and perfect word concerning your life. Fulfilling your purpose means living your life in agreement with His plan. God's plans are unique and individually specific, yet they are always a part of His greater vision. For some the fulfillment of their purpose will bring status, wealth, and fame while others won't have such visible assets. You can fulfill God's plan for your life whether you are a millionaire or middle class. The power you possess to affect lives is unlimited. When you fulfill

God's purpose for your life, it bears the fruit of righteousness. You will live a life of power, peace, and contentment. Some people perform tasks and receive fame, fortune, and reputation but still miss the mark of fulfilling their divine mission in life. Spiritually maturing Christians aim to please God by fulfilling His will.

Fulfilling your purpose should never be confused with material gain. God didn't say that performance equals purpose. Fulfilling your purpose is about fulfilling God's mandate for your life. It means being exactly who God created you to be in the earth. When He looked upon your life, He knew what mark He wanted your life to leave here. You are called to sow your life. You plant your life in the earth in confidence that at the appropriate time your fruit will come forth. God's vision is to have a creation that reflects His glory. The creation was ordained to express the power, authority, and power of God in the earth. So then our purpose here on earth is like that of a prism. A prism receives light and refracts it. Believers receive light from God and refract it into the earth. The light that comes from the believer is sent out like a spectrum, accomplishing all that God desires.

Genesis 1:27-28 is the foundation for purpose in the earth. God created man, both male and female, in His own image. He blessed them and gave them instruction to be fruitful, multiply, and replenish the earth and subdue it. He told them to have dominion over the waters, the skies, and every living thing that moves on the earth. It was and still remains quite an amazing purpose. The book of Revelation adds that God created all things for His pleasure. When a believer is fulfilling his purpose on earth, it brings God pleasure. It's not a particular job that has glory attached to it but the job designed for you. The right fit brings peace and joy in living. It creates a life where you consistently worship God by being fruitful, multiplying, and replenishing the earth. It allows you to subdue and have dominion. This brings glory to the name of the Lord. Sometimes man is too self-absorbed. Pursuing purpose is about God's definition of you. It is about what He says He wants from you and looking at the gifts, talents, and abilities He has given you to get those things in the earth. Purpose is about God. You are the vessel through which God's purpose and plan for the earth is brought to fruition.

> The heart is more deceitful than all else and is desperately sick; who can understand it? I, the Lord search the heart; I test the mind, even to give each man according to his ways, according to the results of his deeds.
>
> Jeremiah 17:9-10

In pursuing purpose, your heart must be purified. There cannot be any evidence of double-mindedness. You must fully believe God and have a passion for seeing His vision come to pass. Your belief in the vision causes you to follow and obey. Submission and obedience spring from a firm confidence and trust in the power of God.

Addressing Spiritual Myths

Myth 1: Fulfilling my purpose will make me well-known, rich, and successful

Society teaches that those who are in the spotlight have made it. My question is, made it to where? We are often faced with the dysfunction of our own vision when we think of fulfilling our purpose. Everyone has thoughts about their million-dollar idea: "If I can just do this...I'll make it big." We narrowly define the scope of our purpose by what it can produce for us, meaning money, status, and prestige. Subtly, we have been taught to think the ultimate in fulfilling purpose is to win. We see it on the playing fields, we see it on award shows, and we see it all around us. Unfortunately, what we don't see is how these images and attitudes have shaped our personal vision regarding purpose and performance.

In essence, it becomes very difficult to remain hopeful, focused, and jubilant if you believe that fulfilling your purpose must equate to wealth, recognition, and status. The highest aim of your purpose is not to produce for you but for God.

Myth 2: Fulfilling my purpose should be easy

The here lies in how "easy" is defined. Jesus fulfilled His purpose in the earth, and it was not was not easy at all. There is nothing easy about being nailed to a cross; nevertheless, He did it.

Although we have a tendency to want things quick, fast, and way it does not always happen that way. Be careful that a sense of entitlement does not derail your pursuit of purpose. Often on the road to becoming all God ordained you will encounter difficulties. Romans 8:28, reminds us that all things do work together for the good of those that love the Lord and are called according to His purpose. Therefore encountering difficulties is nothing more than a stepping-stone to the place God has for you.

Ultimately, your purpose connects you to the fulfillment of God's plan. God never guaranteed your road would be easy but He did guarantee He would never leave you. Your divinely designed path, whether it is easy or rough, culti-vates the fruit of Spirit that you may be the most effective at fulfilling your purpose.

Do not think that fulfilling your purpose will easy. If you think like this, you may be tempted to give up too soon. Life shows us that it always seems the hardest right before the victory. Do not allow this myth to keep you from fulfilling all God planned for you. Remember, purpose is not primarily about you, it is about God. When you encounter difficulties along the way, know that God is still with you and you will prevail.

Myth 3: I can use my talent to become successful, thereby fulfilling purpose

No one can deny that there are a lot of talented people in the world. The exercise of their talent is not their gift from God.

You cannot circumvent God, use the gifts He gave you, and then believe you are fulfilling purpose. Many people take the gifts, skills, and talents they have and put them to use. The result can often be success, at least by the world's standard. They receive recognition, honor, and money yet remain unfulfilled, lacking peace and contentment.

Discovering your talent, gift, or skill and putting it to use by your own methods does not equal purpose. Talented people come and go but God gives longevity. Not only that, but the fruit that comes from a divine gift will remain. It will be the healing of the nations.

Think about it for a minute. Have you ever heard of "one hit wonders"? The people who make this list did something—released an album or song that struck it big—but they were never able to repeat the pattern. That's the difference between performance and purpose. The principles that are tied to fulfilling purpose are reproducible. They didn't just work one time and then you have to try over again to produce the same results.

Imparting Spiritual Truth

Truth 1: Fulfilling purpose will bring you peace, contentment, favor, and eternal reward

The spiritual blessings we gain from fulfilling our purpose far surpass those of the world. Our measure of success is different from that of the world. Success by the world's standard is often equated with money, fame, and recognition. For the believer, those things may come, but they are not the motivating factors, nor are they the true measure of success in God's eyes. As we travel the road of faith, we must open our eyes to spiritual success. On the other hand, it is important to recognize that God does not place a prohibition on earning money or gaining wealth. Christian spirituality is not measured by the abundance or lack of wealth. Guard against the thought that those who have wealth cannot be spiritual as well as the thought that those who lack it are more spiritual than others.

The measure of success of a truly spiritual life is found in the richness of humility, fellowship with the Father, and wisdom. Money is not evil, but the love of money is the root of all evil. God doesn't have a problem with your purpose positioning you to acquire money. Money is a tool in the believer's hand to expand the kingdom. It does not bring peace; only God brings peace. Beyond the money are the true joy, satisfaction, and contentment that come from knowing your life is being lived according to God's plan. Fulfilling purpose causes you to find contentment. Contentment is to honestly and gratefully recognize that God is sovereign over your life, and wherever you find yourself is due to the sovereign power of God. Paul said, "I have learned to be content in whatsoever state I find myself." Contentment is a certainty when you are fulfilling purpose.

Another aspect of truth revealed when you are pursuing purpose is that of grace. The grace of God resting upon you helps to steady you and provide unique equipping for your work. God's grace, or unmerited favor, toward you will help you in times of need. Grace is a helper. Don't confuse grace with mercy. Grace is the unmerited favor of God while mercy is the help/ assistance of God when you should have experienced some harsh consequence instead.

God's favor or grace upon you is a blessing in the pursuit of all you do toward your purpose. It empowers you to stand.

It restores hope in times of despair. God's grace propels you as you seek to fulfill purpose. The effect of God's grace on you is remarkable. Recognizing that your ability is being enhanced by the Creator of the universe is only more fuel. God's grace is sufficient when you feel that you can't go on. His grace continues to move you along the path of accomplishment. Grace is like being empowered to complete a work you thought you couldn't do while mercy is the call to do it after missing the mark. It is a necessary component of your life as you pursue purpose. Grace keeps the path lubricated with peace because challenges will be faced. Contentment is a necessary ingredient as it helps us to rejoice in all situations and circumstances.

Truth 2: Fulfilling your purpose may take effort
The report has never been that life is easy. Fulfilling your purpose will take effort on your part. But you don't have to fear because God is there and will do more than you could ever imagine, ensuring that you accomplish the work you set out to do. If your purpose in life is to become a doctor, you must go to school, study, and make good choices. Accomplishing such a task takes effort. There is no shortcut to the medical degree. In a world filled with methods to get it done quicker, resist the urge to gain without going through the process. The process itself is valuable. We must fight the desire to gain things easily and without effort. Our society is definitely not conducive to this point. We live in a world with a great emphasis on "get rich quick" schemes and getting something for little or nothing tricks. Sometimes things happen quickly. Most of the time what seems quick to those on the outside has meant hours, weeks, months, or even years of labor and preparation to achieve the visible result. As believers we cannot ascribe to the thinking that things must happen quickly. We must be willing to work through the process. Truth be told, many would like to get a college

degree without hours of study and preparation, or have the fruit of a successful business without the daily demands and work involved in attaining it, but this is not God's way. In order to reap you must sow. Fulfilling your purpose will take effort, commitment, and consistency on your part.

God's part is intrinsically tied to our effort. When we begin to work the Spirit of the Lord is quickened and we can expect to receive the benefits of the Holy Spirit working in our life. One of the Holy Spirit's jobs is to bring all things back to your remembrance that the Lord has spoken to you. So as you work you will be reminded of why you're doing it, and that will encourage and empower you to keep going. God didn't say it would be easy but He did say He would be your Helper.

Truth 3: Using your gifts and talents doesn't bring eternal reward unless they are surrendered to God

The gifts and calling of God are without repentance. God gave gifts to every man. He has issued a call to every man, the call to salvation and purpose. It is important to recognize that all we have comes from God, and that means the Creator knows exactly the best use for them. Many people have skills and talents and use them to make a name for themselves. Yet when you surrender your life to God, He empowers and equips you to use your gifts in the service of expanding His kingdom. You may in fact become well-known but that is secondary to the mission. Gifts used in the service of God edify the kingdom, glorify His name, and bring others to a clearer knowledge of Him. Gifts used in the service of self have no eternal value or reward. Spiritual living is the result of opening our eyes and seeing that every gift, skill, or talent has an eternal purpose before the Lord. When we truly comprehend this we will cease to do it our own way and remain faithful to God's way. Recognizing that your gifts, skills, and talents must be surrendered to the will of God will help you launch your ship in the proper direction of fulfilling the will of God.

There is another important aspect of performance and purpose that must be explored. If we are to truly fulfill purpose, spiritual stability is required. This means a true conversion experience combined with a healthy respect for the power of God.

Truth 4: Your past actions are an indication of what lies within you

Your past actions show you what motivates you and what you need to watch out for. They show you what your predilections are (a predilection speaks of an attitude of mind that predisposes one to favor something). A predilection doesn't necessarily have to be a bad thing. In fact, it can be good. The question is never one of whether something is good. The only question is whether or not it is of God. From the beginning of time, we were never to concern ourselves with whether we could distinguish good and evil but that we followed God. We must live not by what we perceive to be the good choice but by the God choice, for God would not lead us to anything wrong. However, we may not be able to see the good in a thing from our vantage point. Sometimes predilections get us in trouble.

In trying to understand the misconceptions about performance and purpose, a study of Simon the sorcerer in the eighth chapter of Acts might prove helpful. Simon was a man who made a living working witchcraft. He tried to profit from sharing illegally accessed information and power. He practiced magic. Sometimes believers practice magic too. He used his own means and methods to change the natural course of events for his own benefit. Magic can be defined as the imposition of man's will on a higher authority.

Simon's predilection was to be self-centered. He used control and manipulation to glorify himself. His actions resulted in people following him, adoring him, and ascribing to him power and recognition. If Simon had not gotten the desired results from the actions he performed, he would have stopped. This helps us to see that if we are getting our needs met then stopping an action may be difficult. This remains true at least until we face our inward desires, deny them, and take up the mind of Christ. It becomes a non-issue when we realize that it is not about us anyway but about God. It is not about your personal kingdom but about the kingdom of God. Simon's second desire was to be popular and to have others think highly of him.

Why must we see this in terms of purpose? First, because you will convince yourself of your purpose based on what it does for you and not what it does for others. You may be quite successful but you can miss the mark and not truly experience the benefits of salvation. Second, you need to be aware of your predispositions are so that you are note entangled in them — it helps you develop and keep a healthy attitude.

It is also important to be aware that the things we find appealing do not necessarily translate into purpose either. People believed Simon. People who do not know the truth are often amazed by that which seems miraculous but is not real. It's possible to get caught up in what others think about your performance. We know it was performance-based and not purpose-based because people believed in him, but no lasting spiritual fruit was produced. Simon was even struck by the truth. He believed Philip, was baptized, and followed. Yet we find that his conversion may not have been real. The text implies that he was amazed by Philip's ability to perform signs and therefore he followed. See, you have to stop and say, "Do I believe in the sign or do I believe in the God behind the sign?"

Simon saw the apostles perform a miraculous thing by imparting the Holy Spirit through the laying on of hands, and he wanted that power. This shows us that he had not given up his old predilections and was drawn away from the Lord by his own lust. The book of James says, *"Let no man say when he is tempted of evil that he is tempted by God but he is drawn away by his own lust that when lust conceived springs forth as sin."* (James 1:13)

If you fail to explore those predilections and how they deeply affect you, you can still be dominated by those actions and miss the gift of salvation. Simon asked for the power/authority and offered the apostles money. Why? Because he wanted to what they did, so people would again recognize him and honor him. It wasn't about God; it was about his self-centered motives that had led him to become the magician of Samaria.

You can mentally assent to the truth, but until your actions line up with that truth you have not fully believed. Simon was engulfed in bitterness. He had been the ruling magician, and he wanted to be on par with Philip. He thought he was worthy of honor. He wanted to be recognized. He wanted to be adored. It wasn't about God. It was about him and his personal desire for power. He believed his work made him great and failed to realize that the power of God is greater than everything. This is why Peter rebuked him for having rebellion in his heart. Don't fall into the trap of thinking performance equals purpose. Seek God with your whole heart and know that pursuing purpose brings with it great spiritual rewards.

God's View

You were created to live a life designed by God. Your life is to be one of purpose, peace, and passion. Not only does your life have meaning to those around you but it is designed to have a profound impact in expanding the kingdom.

In God's view, the only success that merits anything is that which is born out of our proper relationship with the Father. Recall that Matthew 7:23 tells the story of the workers coming to Jesus expecting a reward. They had come about doing the work of the Lord—healing the sick, casting out demons, all under the authority of the name of Jesus— yet when Jesus spoke He called them workers of iniquity because they lacked relationship with Him. Relationship with God is essential as when in pursuit of purpose.

That relationship must be born out of love and culti- vated through the seeds of purity, obedience, and submis- sion. Fulfilling your divine purpose springs forth out of your body when your being has been chastened enough to despise self-absorption. Pursuing purpose is to live by and adhere to God's definition of you. He has created you to *be* before you *do*. God says you are, and out of that will flow the magnificent power of purpose fulfilled. When you choose to embrace *being* over *doing,* you prove to the world that God did not say performance equals purpose.

Renew Your Mind...

Think about the previous chapter. What challenged your thinking in this area? Take a moment and interact with the material by journaling your thoughts prior to reading and your thoughts now.

_____
_____
_____
_____
_____
_____
_____
_____
_____
_____

Transform Your Walk...

Change occurs when we move from thinking to doing. Change involves action. In what ways or areas of your life have you considered performance to be equal with purpose?

_____
_____
_____
_____
_____
_____
_____
_____
_____
_____

Chapter Five

God Didn't Say...Have It Your Way

"Delight thyself also in the Lord; and he shall give thee the desires of thine heart." Psalm 37:4

Setting the Stage

Growing up, I remember a slogan that said "Have it your way." The franchise that coined the slogan wanted its customer to know they could have their sandwich any way they wanted. The point of the slogan was that you know what you like. It was their job to give it to you. So they set out to appeal to your natural desire to do things your own way. It was probably genius from their perspective but hazardous to the worldview of a Christian. When it comes to a meal "having it your way" is acceptable, but when that thinking creeps into your daily living and permeates other areas of your spiritual walk, you have a problem.

The influence of culture on our attitudes and behaviors can cause great difficulty when we try to deepen our relationship with the Father. Too often, we try to take thoughts, ideas, and patterns established in the world and incorporate them into our faith walk. This does not always lead to spiritual success and gratification. Friendship with the world is enmity with God. God's ways are higher and different from ours.

Success and prosperity of soul and spirit happens as life is lived according to the culture of heaven and the kingdom of God, not the fallen world. Embracing the thinking that you can have it your way keeps you from obeying and submitting to the Word of God. In order to grow, prosper, and fulfill your purpose in the earth you must be willing to relinquish your will and accept the will of God as your own. In order to accept God's will, spiritual strongholds must be torn down. Eradicating the strongholds and embracing God's way begins when you take a look at the walls erected in your life and begin to dismantle them. Sounds easy enough, but let's take a holistic look at the spiritual myths that create strongholds around this issue.

A spiritual stronghold is a place that has been established or fortified to keep thoughts, behaviors, or attitudes safe. Spiritually speaking this is beyond a physical dwelling or edifice. It can be a thought, argument, or combination of things that keep a believer from experiencing the freedom God desires for them. Paul addresses it in 2 Corinthians 10:4-5: *"(For the weapons of our warfare are not carnal, but mighty through God to the pulling down of strongholds;) casting down imaginations, and every high thing that exalteth itself against the knowledge of God, and bringing into captivity every thought to the obedience of Christ."*

It is imperative that strongholds be brought down and your thoughts, ideas, and imaginations come in line with the Word of God. Alignment is the result of proper choices made. Examine your mind to comprehend what spiritual fortifications might be keeping you from surrendering to the Lord.

Addressing Spiritual Myths
Myth 1: If I ask for anything in the name of Jesus
I will get it

Most of the time the phrase "in the name of Jesus," is used just like magicians use "Abracadabra!" It is tacked on to the end of prayer with an expectation that now something miraculous will happen. There seems to be little regard for the true meaning of praying in the name of Jesus. Jesus did say we should ask in His name and according to his will. He did say, you would receive but we must also understand the conditions placed upon asking and receiving. To ask in the name of Jesus is not simply adding a mystical incantation but to clearly understand the power, authority, and purpose of Jesus the Christ. When you pray "in the name of Jesus," you are aware of the person and the work of Jesus Christ in relation to the plan of God for humanity. You stand in full agreement with that plan. When you pray "in the name of Jesus," you are invoking the power and authority of God based on the work of Jesus Christ.

Many believe they will receive anything they ask for as long as they ask "in the name of Jesus." There is very little thought given to the proper context of asking in His name. Thinking that anything we need, want, or pray for will be ours because we say "in the name of Jesus" is akin to manipulation. The phrase does not make God melt like butter. It is not a magic bullet. God never intended us to think of it this way and when we do those thoughts and prayers are unfruitful and leave you disappointed. God is not a genie in a lamp, and your spiritual walk cannot be based on magical incantations or other trickery to receive power. God is not a wish-granting sugar daddy. He is the sovereign Creator who created all things for His pleasure and has a magnificent plan for His creation. He has a magnificent plan for you.

You may think that this myth does not affect you because you do not verbally say "in the name of Jesus when you pray. Although your actions may not reflect it, your thoughts about praying "in the name of Jesus" may still be imprinted on your heart. Just remember God knows our hearts. He does not look or judge based on the surface. Just because you do not say something openly does not mean that God doesn't know exactly what our motivations are. Believing this myth can lead to great disillusionment and a lack of consistency in your faith walk. When you believe you can ask for anything you desire and receive it without fail, you have missed the mark regarding the character and nature of God. God loves us with an everlasting love. His love, known as agape love, is the highest expression of His character and nature. Agape love, derived from the Greek word *agapao*, is defined as an unconditional or benevolent love. Agape loves doesn't always give what is desired but what is deemed best. Agape love implies that the one who loves is unselfish, compassionate, and wise enough to know what the one loved needs.

Myth 2: God will give me the desires of my heart

Modern translation: "God will grant me whatever I can think of and place in my heart." This is very similar in tone to myth one. This statement actually sets up a different stronghold that must be addressed. Jeremiah 17:9 says, *"The heart is deceitful above all things, and desperately wicked: who can know it?"* The response given is found in verse 10, *"I the Lord search the heart, I try the reins, even to give every man according to his way, and according to the fruit of his doings."* Many times the things that come from our heart are not springing forth from God but from our own desires. Our desires tend to satisfy, strengthen, or enliven us. Our desires are firmly bound up in our personal comfort, satisfaction, or peace. Yes, righteousness does not spring from us but it precipitates from God. He tells us in Psalm 37:4, *"Delight thyself also in the Lord: and he shall give thee the desires of thine heart."* This scripture teaches us that when we find joy, peace, and satisfaction in serving and knowing the Lord, He will begin to place the proper desires in us. Belief that God will grant every desire of our heart places us in a position of being cut off from His promise to fill our heart, mind, and soul with good things. God will satisfy us with good things, yet we must recognize that every good and perfect gift comes from above, from the Father of Lights, with whom there is no shadow of turning (see James 1:17).

Myth 3: You can ask for anything and everything

Many think all you have to do is ask God, believe in what you want, and He will grant every request. This amounts to nothing more than reducing God to the image of the "great sugar daddy of the sky," waiting around to fulfill personal whims. Believing this myth opens the door to developing a way of thinking that dismisses the need for personal responsibility. God didn't say that a powerful spiritual life would be experienced without the assertion of personal responsibility. Nor did He say believe in what you want. Always place your faith in God not in your ability to believe what you want. If you are not careful, this myth will cause you to have difficulty discerning the object of your faith. Your faith should be firmly in God. When it is in God, He gives you the desires of your heart and you receive all that He has for you. When it is not in God, but in what you want disappointment is probably imminent. Job, even through His suffering and trials was confident in God. Abraham was counted righteous because his faith was in God. Don't sabotage your right to having all that God ordains for you by only desiring to have things your way.

Myth 4: Believe it, receive it, it's yours

There is hardly a more used statement than this one. You might frequently hear it following a prayer or petition where someone asks, "You believe God right?" To which most people answer, "Yes." The inference is that since you believe it you will get it. Somewhere the thought pattern here is off, we fall into thinking, believing in what I want is more powerful than believing in God. Faith in God is the key not faith in your desire. When we have faith in God, we recognize that He knows what is best for us and we trust Him to give or withhold according His plan. We must accept that faith in God is the standard and obedience is the key. It is also important not to neglect personal responsibility. In order to move beyond this myth you must first recognize that God answers prayer according to His will and not simply the desires that come from man's heart. Jeremiah 17:9 reminds us that the heart is desperately wicked and no man can know it; but God tries the reins of the heart and rewards every man according to their doing. Two points here, one sometimes our hearts can deceive us; and two, rewards don't necessarily have to positive. The second thing that must be recognized is the personal responsibility theme seems to show up again. The point is salient to the same scripture mentioned above, Matthew 21:22, but you can also read 1 John 3:22 to gain insight. It is true enough that an act of faith causes things to happen, yet God tied a few additional strings to the baton that carries the answer to our prayers: *"And whatsoever we ask, we receive of him, because we keep his commandments, and do those things that are pleasing in his sight" (1 John 3:22).* The matter of believing and receiving everything we desire must be broken in our hearts if we are to renew our minds and transform our lives. God has tied obedience to believing and receiving, which supports the premise that God responds to that which comes from Him.

Each of the four myths lends itself to the creation of strongholds that keep us from experiencing the freedom of God. Strongholds can cause years of spiritual languishing. The challenge is that each myth can create a tangled web of deception and confusion. Deception and confusion are precursors to death. If you want to dismantle the power of death in your spiritual walk, you must first bind the strong man. The strong man is revealed through the erroneous beliefs about having it your way that keep you bound. The way to recovery is to receive the facts.

Imparting Spiritual Truth
Truth 1: God's way is better than your way

Proverbs 3:5-6 says, *"Trust in the Lord with all thine heart; and lean not unto thine own understanding. In all thy ways acknowledge him, and he shall direct thy paths."* Proverbs 14:12 states, *"There is a way which seemeth right unto a man, but the end thereof are the ways of death."* Moreover, Proverbs 12:15 reads, *"The way of a fool is right in his own eyes: but he that hearkeneth unto counsel is wise."*

Essentially, we must be cautious about our desire to have things work out our way, a way that is favorable and beneficial to us. Proverbs warns us that our ways may always seem right in our own sight, yet the Lord weighs the spirit. We must understand that we were never intended to move in the knowledge of good and evil. Consider the fact that God told Adam and Eve they could eat from every tree in the garden except the tree of the knowledge of good and evil. Their eating of that tree opened up a Pandora's Box, causing us to desire to know and understand what seems right to us.

Truth 2: God's way is the best way

Psalm 18:30 says, *"As for God, his way is perfect: the word of the Lord is tried: he is a buckler to all those that trust in him."* As we come to recognize that our hearts, minds, thoughts, and ideas can lead us contrary to the way of God, we must embrace the fact that our ways pale in comparison to God's ways. At best, we want things to be our own way because it seems easy, but easy isn't always best. If you determine that you want to run a marathon, you can take the easy road and hope you will make the distance, or you can take the tough road of training and know that you are strong enough to make the distance.

You must acknowledge that He knows what is best for you, even if it means enduring some difficult places or not having it your way. Jeremiah 29:11 reminds us, *"For I know the thoughts that I think toward you, saith the Lord, thoughts of peace, and not of evil, to give you an expected end."*

The third chapter of Exodus teaches us that it's better to experience the way of the Lord than to be left to our own devices. All of God's ways lead to righteousness while our ways can lead to death. His ways are life and peace.

Truth 3: God is committed to prospering those who choose His way

Deuteronomy 8:6 states, *"Therefore thou shalt keep the commandments of the Lord thy God, to walk in his ways, and to fear him. For the Lord thy God bringeth thee into a good land, a land of brooks of water, of fountains and depths that spring out of valleys and hills."* The ways that seem right to us can take us in a completely different direction than God's. We could ignorantly be choosing death. It's almost like choosing death by default. Be careful of actions that transpire as a default. It can be very different from what you intended. Everyone wants to walk in spiritual prosperity.

Truth 4: Maintain a selfless attitude

The desire to "have it your way" comes from a destructive forces known as pride selfishness, and arrogance but victory comes from an attitude of selflessness. Ultimately, true freedom and deliverance to live according to the Word comes as we accept the fact that our ideas, thoughts, and beliefs must reflect the true nature and character of God. In order to accurately reflect the heart and mind of God, we must exhibit humility. Paul said, "I am crucified with Christ nevertheless I live yet not I but Christ liveth in me: and the life I now live in the flesh I live by the faith of the Son of God, who loved me, and gave himself for me." Galatians 2:20. You must die to self. This means your desire is that God's will be demonstrated and not necessarily your own. You have been crucified with Christ in a very spiritual sense, therefore selfishness, pride, and arrogance should not be a part of your experience. Selflessness is reflected in you ability to live by faith in the word.

Intellectual agreement with that won't bring victory either, if that is all there is—intellectual assent. To agree intellectually that God's ways are better than yours but continue to repeat old actions, thoughts, and behaviors, only diminish your spiritual power. The place of true power is when your agreement with God's way spills over into consistent, righteous action.

God's View

God's view of having it our way is much different from what we think. God speaks to us about our selfishness from His perspective. Our desires without Him are mostly selfish. Yet when we delight ourselves in Him, He gives us the desires of our heart. We must learn to surrender our will and take up the will of God. It is the ultimate act of worship. When you are a true worshipper of God, you learn to say just as Jesus said in the Garden of Gethsemane, "Nevertheless not My will but Thy will be done."

The use of having your way really comes down to will. From God's vantage point, when you are truly ready to accept His way you surrender your will to His. The denial of your own will to the will of God is the highest form of worship.

Renew Your Mind...

Think about having it your way. Can you relate to that desire within yourself? What challenged your thinking in this area? Take a moment and interact with the material by journaling your thoughts prior to reading and your thoughts now.

_____

_____

_____

_____

_____

_____

_____

_____

_____

_____

Transform Your Walk...

Change occurs when we move from thinking to doing. Change involves action. What things do you need to let God have His way in?

_____

_____

_____

_____

_____

_____

_____

_____

_____

_____

_____

Chapter Six

God Didn't Say...
There Would Never Be Pain

"For our light affliction, which is but for a moment,
worketh for us a far more exceeding and eternal weight
of glory." 2 Corinthians 4:17

Setting the Stage

Somewhere along the line, we have come to believe that life in Christ will always be rainbows, butterflies, and lollipops falling from heaven. By that, I mean when times of pain or suffering happen we start to think we've done something to upset God or to bring this situation on ourselves. That may be true to some extent, since our actions do have consequences. Yet it's also true that the normal path of life contains suffering for both believers and unbelievers. Christianity does not make us immune to pain or suffering; instead it sets us free in the midst of hardship as we realize God is sovereign and His love covers us and comforts us through the circumstance.

There are truly times in life when the pain, heartbreak, or disappointment seems too difficult to bear. During those times, we must strive to maintain an attitude of worship.

God didn't promise that every day of our lives would be pain-free. He did not say "come unto Me and I will make you exempt from the human condition." He promised that He would always be there, His love would be comforting, His grace sufficient, and His mercy everlasting. Our ability to triumph during times of pain confirms God's existence. It shows that not only can He be trusted to help us prevail over pain, but also that He will give us strength and heal our wounds. Remember the power of Jesus taking on the form of man and walking the earth. Jesus came to earth and experienced pain. He suffered through the spiritual and natural pain, and through that suffering He learned the power of obedience. He became the perfecter of our faith. Our experience on earth will not differ from His. We can expect to suffer loss. We can expect that some things won't feel so good, but we can definitely count on the fact that God will never leave us nor forsake us. We can celebrate the blessedness of fellowship with God in the midst of every situation. As we embrace this truth, we must open our hearts and minds to release those ideas and imaginations that stand in opposition to God's way.

Addressing Spiritual Myths
Myth 1: If you experience pain, you have sinned

This is the argument Job's friends used in his time of suffering. They were adamant that he must have done something wrong to be in that state. Job's friends subscribed to the line of reasoning that says, "Bad things only happen to bad people." The entire book of Job refutes that faulty notion and magnifies the wisdom of God in all situations—even the ones we don't understand. Bad things happen to all people. No one is immune. Just as good things happen to all people. Yet the best things are reserved for those who love Him.

The problem here is that even if you believe this faulty doctrine on a subconscious level, it will shape the way you view and respond to situations. By accepting this premise, you actually displace the sovereignty of God and put great honor upon yourself. In fact, you have begun to trust in your own righteousness and not that of God. Accepting this myth could lead to wasted time spent searching for something to blame. It leads to excessive guilt and shame. Focusing on yourself rather than on God can give rise to depression. We must allow the words of God to renew our thinking in this area.

Myth 2: If bad things are happening in my life, God is punishing me

Whenever I hear this statement, it brings to mind a picture of the Greek gods of mythology. I can imagine the gods on Mt. Olympus standing around making decisions in response to the actions of men below. The gods were depicted as very reactionary and not proactive. They operated in response to being offended, and they moved in line with their own personal whims, desires, and agendas. The God of Abraham, Isaac, and Jacob does not react that way. He created everything and never has to run around in response to something. His Word has already been established and is always at work to accomplish His will. First, we know that the Greek gods weren't actually real but merely reflected the beliefs of the people at the time. In fact, Elijah came against the prophets of Baal when he ridiculed them on Mt. Carmel, telling the prophets to cry out and scream louder, for maybe their god was asleep!

Believing this myth gives rise to an attitude of self-pity, reduced self-esteem, and victimization. This renders you incapable of walking or standing in power as you deny your identity. Yes, there are times when we do things that displease God, and we must deal with the consequences, but there are also times when we are simply dealing with the effects of sin in the world.

Myth 3: I can avoid all pain if I only live a good enough life

Again, we have neglected the fact that God is sovereign. This means He is in control of all things and all situations. At the heart of this myth is a belief that you have the power to control all that happens to you simply by being good. This too is erroneous thinking and leads to an extremely legalistic outlook. It creates delusion, ignoring the grace of God and the fact that all our righteousness is as filthy rags before Him. Reflecting on the example of Job, he was by all accounts a good and righteous man. His righteousness pleased God, so much so that God even asked Satan, "Are you sure you want to mess with him?" Job lived a good life because he loved God. His good and pious life did not shield him from the issues of pain, loss, and suffering. He suffered physically, mentally, emotionally, and spiritually. In the end he prevailed and received twice what he had in the beginning, but the process he had to endure gives just as much glory and honor to God as the end result.

In the process, we come to know more of God, how He relates to man, and His plan. We learn as Job did that we can trust Him through everything. We are led to acknowledge that God knows better than we do. We confirm our praise and honor of Him. On your spiritual journey, love, kindness, compassion, and service should be integral pieces of your life, but you must also have a healthy attitude about pain and suffering. A holistic view insulates your faith during times of trial. An unhealthy view can cause faith to wither and die.

We must strive to grow in our holiness and righteous living. To take the attitude that being good is an insulator from pain, disappointment, and heartbreak renders us less than functional in society. When you do experience any of these things, you will lose hope and may very well give up the victory because you believe there is nothing else you can do on your part.

Imparting Spiritual Truth

Truth, pain, heartbreak, and suffering are part of the complex human experience. Sin has infected the world, and things happen in the world that affect us. Suffering is not necessarily indicative of personal sin. You must be able to honestly address personal sin in your life and bring your thoughts under the authority of God. Yet when all those things have been dealt with, the truth is that sometimes bad things still happen to good people. It is a part of the human condition. This knowledge can help you to endure the pain. It can cause victory and triumph to prevail as you remember that God is able to do far above what you thought. Though the effects of sin still touch our lives and situations, take heart in knowing that you prevail. God has given you the ability to prevail over all situations. His Word declares that no weapon formed against you shall prosper, and every tongue that rises up in judgment you shall condemn.

Job did not sin and yet lost everything in the midst of his praise, devotion, and honor to God. God has very real spiritual purpose in mind, even in the midst of pain. We cannot avoid pain and suffering in our lives. We can only trust in the sovereignty of God and that ultimately He knows far more than we do and His plan is far superior to ours. A very spiritual fact to consider here is that we are to be witnesses of the power of Jesus Christ on earth. We are to prove the good, perfect, and acceptable will of God. When bad things happen in life that are not the result of personal sin, an opportunity arises for us to demonstrate the veracity of God's Word. We know that we have been given the Comforter (the Holy Spirit). When we are in the midst of difficulties and pain, we do not remain inconsolable. This is a great witness to the operation of God in our lives. It allows us to reveal the will of God on earth.

Enduring challenging circumstances keeps your head lifted, and focusing on the bigger picture is evidence that God is with you. The ultimate benefit of the presence of God with you is that out of victory comes increase and advancement of His kingdom. When we are able to endure circumstances, keep our heads up, and our eyes focused, we prove that we are more than conquerors. We prove that the power of God transcends all circumstances and issues of life. He has given us the key to life and godliness. God has given us the ability to walk in power and authority during difficult times. Circumstances prove that the power and presence of God in your life is greater than anything.

Pain in life doesn't always mean there is personal sin, but victory in the midst of pain always proves there is a God who can be counted on. Many people make it through difficult situations. The difference between doing it with faith-filled perseverance and simple human strength is the spiritual outcome. Spiritual outcomes bring honor to God and reveal Him in the earth. A spiritual outcome may be that others see what you have gone through and are drawn to know more about God. A spiritual outcome can also be that your faith is increased and you are inspired to pursue the path God has set before you. A spiritual outcome may also be an increased production of spiritual fruit in your life. God chastens those whom He loves. Life is not without consequences. To every action there is an equal and opposite reaction—a physics theory. Yet to take the attitude of a victim is to assault your self-esteem.

Job's friends wanted him to accept and believe that God was punishing him for his sin. They begged, pleaded, and sometimes even tried to push him into accepting this premise. Job remained certain of his life and standing. He was at a place where he knew he was doing God's will. What an awesome place to be. He knew that sometimes things happen through no fault of your own. He learned that when things do happen that cause pain, they may have a greater purpose than being sent as some type of punishment. It must be for your good. If it's not chastening because of wrong-doing, it must be allowed as an element to strengthen.

Always consider the fact that the adversary wants you to fall away while the Word of God says, "I have no delight in the death of the unrighteous." The enemy of our souls desires that we reveal unrighteousness, but God proves that that which is inside of us is solid, stable, and incorruptible. Embracing one of the beatitudes here is essential to victory: *Blessed are they who are persecuted for righteousness' sake, for theirs is the kingdom of heaven.* As you mature in your spiritual walk, you will be able to accept God's will with the proper attitude and understanding. You will find peace in the midst of the storm. You will remain faithful to God, trusting Him with the plan of success for your life.

Persecution, pain, and suffering may become a part of our experience for many reasons, but the truth remains that all things do work together for the good of them who love the Lord. Do not allow circumstances to cause you to think like a victim. You are more than a conqueror through Jesus Christ. You can make it through anything.

Consider Shadrach, Meshach, and Abednego. They chose to do the right thing—not bowing to the ways of the world. Subsequently they faced the highest level of punishment, the fiery furnace. They didn't do anything wrong in the eyes of God, yet off to the fiery furnace they were sent because they had offended man. If they had fallen victim to the faulty reasoning that God was punishing them for doing something wrong, perhaps they would have just decided to bow to the king, or perhaps their faith would not have been as strong as they made their steps toward the furnace. It was not a light thing to reject the edict of Nebuchadnezzar, but their faith told them they should please God no matter the outcome.

They didn't run from pain or consequences; they accepted it as reality. Yet through everything they realized that God was sufficient and it was better to endure punishment than to depart from the way of the Lord. It proved quite valuable for them in that they manifested true faith and trust in the Lord. Not only did they survive the punishment, but the Son of Man went through it with them and they prevailed.

Not running from difficult situations but standing on the Word of God advances the influence of the kingdom. Therefore, it is when we must endure heartbreak, pain, disappointment, and persecution. Keeping the right attitude of reverence and worship toward God will give us a victorious experience. We must believe that God will be right there with us in the midst of every affliction. Our victory and prosperity are guaranteed. God's promise is that He will never leave us nor forsake us, no matter where we find ourselves. Even in the midst of pain and persecution.

The story of Daniel provides further proof that living a good life does not insulate you from pain, disappointment, heartbreak, and persecution. Daniel was a praying man. He took his relationship with God very seriously. He diligently sought the Father three times a day. He acknowledged God and adhered to His Word, so much so that others resented him for it. Some might ask, if he was such a good man, why did God allow him to be taken captive to Babylon? Why was he thrown in the lions' den? Why was the answer to his prayer delayed for twenty-one days? Well, it was not because his life was wrecked with personal sin; it was because God had a plan. Daniel had it all together. He honored God. He had an excellent spirit. He possessed a spirit of wisdom. He did not waver in his commitment to the Lord. In fact, his faithfulness and commitment increased through the pain. This helped propel him to the place God desired him to be in order to fulfill His plan. In our lives, we must recognize that everything is purposeful. We as believers are the recipients of the promise of Romans 8:28, *"And we know that all things work together for good to them that love God, to them who are the called according to his purpose."* Pain in your life may come without warning and through no fault of your own, yet the plan of God is to allow it to work for your good and not your destruction. Trust Him.

God's View

We must keep an accurate view of pain. We are not meant to be driven by our emotions or live a reactionary life. God has a plan for our lives. His plan is not set aside because of the entrance of pain. The entrance of pain into the complex equation of a Christian life provides fertile ground for the will of God to manifest. Our experience seeks to help others experience the greatness of God. God desires to use our lives to show a dark and dying world that His way is the answer to the issue of sin, and for His children to experience a life where purpose and passion meet.

Every day might not be the greatest in your estimation, but every day that you are yielded to God and honoring Him is perfect in His estimation. The pain that comes with living in this world is real, yet we stand upon God's Word in every situation and demonstrate His truth. Know that the truth of God's Word prevails. We are able to smile and live with purpose because our eyes have seen greater purpose in the whole arena of life. When we experience the pain of persecution even though we have done nothing wrong, it is an opportunity to prove that God is our great Savior and deliverer. Heartbreak allows us to demonstrate that God is the mender of broken hearts.

Pain transforms you. It opens your eyes and heart to God. It increases your level of humility because through pain you learn that God is true and real. You learn that the things He said He can do are real. Your experience of His comfort, protection, and joy position you for great steps of faith in the future. God didn't say there would never be pain, but He promised that our deliverance from pain would reveal His glory in us. Ultimately, pain provides for transformation in our lives. It brings us to a place of greater confidence in God's faithfulness. It also seeks to establish the truth and power of the kingdom of God on earth.

Renew Your Mind...

Think about the previous chapter. What challenged your thinking in this area? Take a moment and interact with the material by journaling your thoughts prior to reading and your thoughts now.

_____
_____
_____
_____
_____
_____
_____
_____
_____

Transform Your Walk...

Change occurs when we move from thinking to doing. Change involves action. What have your thoughts about pain and difficulties been up to this point? What ideas do you need to let go of in order to have a correct view of pain and suffering and grow in your spiritual walk?

_____
_____
_____
_____
_____
_____
_____
_____
_____
_____

Chapter Seven

God Didn't Say...Love Is Negotiable

*"A new commandment I give unto you, That ye love one
another; ad I have loved you, that ye also love one another.
By this shall all men know that ye are my disciples, if ye
have love one to another"*
John 13:34-35

Setting the Stage

During the early years of working in ministry, I was
teaching a class when a young woman made the
comment that you can love at a distance. A little stunned by
the comment, I asked her to explain. She said, "We won't
like everybody, but we can just tolerate them." I went on to
share with her that loving at a distance is not an option in the
kingdom of God. At what distance does God place His love
toward us?

The Bible declares that God is love. Love is His nature.
He is love and demonstrates that love in everything He does.
The words "I love you" can be three of the most powerful
words in any language. It seems that when we use those
words, things happen. If we say those words to someone
and they reciprocate, we want to do things for them, and if

we say those words to someone and they don't reciprocate, we are hurt and angry. The word *love* has such power that it can cause complete elation or great despair. Human love is often misunderstood and misdirected. Our understanding and appropriation of love flows from the Father's perspective, not ours. Yet the word really denotes a need in each of us. Each of us desires to love and be loved. This need and a lack of understanding it can destroy lives, families, communities, and churches. When you don't know that you were created to desire the love of God and that His love completes you, you start looking for love in all the wrong places. You begin to compromise your dignity for some form of love that is counterfeit. You begin to seek attention from people who don't know what is best for you. You start to believe that self-gratification is the answer.

Conversely, if your life has been void of love or you have been hurt, then you build a wall that says "I don't need anything or anyone...I am okay by myself." All of these pathologies can be destructive. They can cause great damage and hinder your spiritual life.

Let me put it to you clearly. God created you in His likeness and image. You were created to receive *true* love and give *true* love. The challenge is that giving and receiving love is based solely on God's definition, not our human experience. When we try to construct a theology of love based on our own worldview, we lose. Your body knows this, your mind knows this, your heart knows this, and your will knows this. Love is the foundation to spiritual growth. Both the New and Old Testaments provide confirming evidence of the importance of love:

> And thou shalt love the Lord thy God with all thine heart, and with all thy soul, and with all thy might.
> Deuteronomy 6:5

Thou shalt love the Lord thy God with all thy heart,
and with all thy soul, and with all thy mind.
Matthew 22:37

Because of the foundational nature of love, the command
to love is the most powerful one we know. Since there is no
greater command, there is no greater assault to its manifestation. Love is the most powerful emotion on the planet. It is
stronger than hate. It has greater influence and a far-reaching
effect. It is what causes us to be saved. Many people think
that hate is stronger because it is so destructive, but love
outweighs hate. Love reigns over hate.

In our improper attempts to understand, receive, and
give love we develop patterns that destroy the spiritual life.
To work in the power of God's love and experience it on
a personal level, our view of love must be congruent with
God's view. Our minds must be renewed to the concept of
love, its demonstration, and its acceptance in our lives.

Addressing Spiritual Myths

When our God-given need for love has not been met by
Him, it causes many negative behaviors such as promiscuity,
suicide, divorce, depression, debt, etc. All these actions are
a result of not having or receiving God's love. Yet there is
a solution to these issues of life, and I declare that the solution is Jesus Christ. Jesus is the supplier of our needs. He is
more than just an image in our heads. He is more than just
someone we call upon in our times of trouble. You know His
Word is life. How can you say you believe the things of God
yet not completely trust His Word?

In order to position ourselves to operate in love we
must come to Christ and receive Him. Our experience is
not unlike the woman at the well. This story shows us that
there is a place we all get to in life where we must make a
choice. The Samaritan woman faced the choice of receiving

natural water or spiritual water. We have the same choice today. Do we receive natural water or spiritual water? More specifically, will we receive natural love or spiritual love? Natural love isn't eternally satisfying—the love of Jesus is completely satisfying.

Today, Jesus is sitting by the well of Sychar, and He is waiting on you, His next appointment. The disciples have left to go purchase meat, but He waits for you. He waits for you to come to that place where you are trying to refill your bucket with all you have had before, going through the same old thing again and again. He sits at the place where you go to get the same water time and time again. The concept of love we carry sometimes sends us back to the well. Relationships are never satisfying enough, nor do they last long enough. We come back to the well to get some more of the same, believing that's all we can have, but God wants to give you spiritual water—love that will change your actions. His love will cause you to be an asset to the kingdom. His love will reveal the deficiency of your past but inspire you to embrace the hope and perfection of His plan.

First of all, notice that Jesus was already at the well. You don't have to look very far for Him; He knows where you are going and when He needs to meet with you. He will be right there. You only have to see Him. You have to recognize Him. Jesus was already at the well. God wants you to know that His love crosses all barriers: racial, social, gender, cultural, and religious. It stands the test of time and closes the gap. You do not love at a distance. Jesus crossed all barriers to get the truth to this woman. He broke the gender barrier, the cultural barrier, the religious barrier, and the racial barrier to reach her. What kind of love is that?

She responded by challenging His ability to cross the lines that were firmly established in her society. She asked Him, "How is it that you are asking me for a drink?" She was saying, *You shouldn't even ask me that. It is not right.*

She was operating from a standpoint of putting God in a box. How often does God try to cross barriers with us and we put Him right back in the box of our own thinking? Our carnal thinking causes us to believe that God can't ask us to give up everything. *You can't be asking me to sacrifice that thing.*

Sometimes God will ask you for something that you can't supply on your own. He will call you out of your comfort zone. This happens to bring you to the place where you will put your trust in Him. God is a tremendous confidence builder. Sometimes we look at a situation and say to Jesus, "Look, you don't even have the right stuff and the situation is deep." We always want proof of something. We want to know that what He has is greater for us than what we have now. We must understand that ultimately eternity is greater than what we have.

It's not a matter of better it's a matter of God. Do not miss the point. The water God gives is eternally satisfying. This water rises up in you. It shall be in you a well springing up into everlasting life. Jesus waits for us to ask Him for the water. In the Gospel of John chapter 4 verse 15, the Samaritan woman asks for the water. She confesses her desire to never thirst again and not have to travel back to that place where He met her.

At that point, Jesus asked her to go get her husband. No, he wasn't saying "I can only deal with a woman if her husband is with her." He was calling her to address her life situation. She had no true, lasting love relationship. It is impossible to build a strong, true covenant relationship without the love of Jesus. Her answer, "I have no husband," was the truth. Jesus showed her, "You are truthful, now let Me address your sources. You tried five other sources to get this living water you desire, but they were not right and now you are on your sixth source, and he is not right either. You haven't even attempted to enter covenant with him. So you see that your sources have been wrong. You have been in error." Verses 28-30 show us that after you have received the living water, you want to share what happened and encourage others to go and get the same thing.

Jesus wants to meet us at the well. The well of our past issues, relationships, concerns, hurts, thoughts, behaviors, ways of doing things—He even wants to meet us at the place where we do ministry and say to us, "I am the living water." Will you accept His offer?

Addressing spiritual myths will help move you into victory.

Myth 1: Love is conditional

Although we say love should be unconditional, our attitudes and actions portray another story. We place conditions on our love relationships when we try to get people to do what we want before we will give them love.

Love is unconditional. You must realize that love is not material things. Love isn't even your presence or your time. You give these things because you love, not because they define love. First Corinthians 13 teaches us that love is the fundamental element of all that we do. Somehow we have come to believe that what we do is love. The truth is what we do *should* be based on or spring from love. Love has some very deliberate characteristics: patience, kindness, longsuffering, thinking no evil; not envious, jealous, boastful, or proud. Yet how often do we demonstrate these characteristics in our love relationships? When we believe ourselves to be completely immersed in love, how many of these characteristics are in full operation? Can the purity of your love be seen in the tapestry of all your relationships?

Myth 2: Speaking the truth in love means saying whatever I want to say

This little myth can cause you to lose the victory. We have been taught that as long as we believe our actions are honest, we bear no responsibility to the other individual. We believe that if we tell ourselves we are doing something out of love, it must be true. Most of the time we do things from a self-serving or critical vantage point.

Many relationships are damaged because someone purported to be speaking the truth in love. Again, when we are ready to say something to someone, the characteristics of love must be evident in that conversation.

Imparting Truth
Truth vs. Honesty

The Bible teaches us that when we know and continue in the truth, it will make us free. Speaking the truth has a powerful effect on the hearer, not just on the one delivering the message. The word of truth causes faith to increase. When faith increases transformation takes place. Most times we are far less concerned with the truth than we are with honesty.

Many would say there is no difference between truth and honesty, but that is not so. Honesty can be very subjective while the truth that comes from the Word of God is not subjective. It is objective and defining. The truth has the power to set men free. The truth has the power to change a person's manner of living. It has the power to change the way a person thinks. Honesty has the power to fulfill self. Don't get me wrong. I am not discarding the virtue of honesty, just bringing to light that truth transcends honesty. In kingdom thinking, it is the next level.

For example, a husband and wife may have a disagreement. The wife says, "I honestly felt that you didn't love me when we disagreed on that." The truth is his love for her never changed just because of a little disagreement. Disagreements tend to give rise to the revelation of truth. We might honestly feel we are not worthy of God's love and forgiveness. The truth is that through the work of Jesus Christ, we are counted worthy.

Society, and even the church, has taught us that we can say anything we want to say to someone as long as we add this little catchphrase. How many times has an honest comment damaged someone? It is better to tell the truth and be cautious with your words than to satisfy your own desire and hurt someone.

Truth 1: Love is unconditional

The word for God's love is agape. His love seeks to give us all that we need for life, strength, and success. God's love meets our needs beyond anything that we could imagine. You must believe that God wants the best for you and that all His work as well as His daily provision is about bringing His best to your life. He loves you at all times. It is not based on you but on His righteousness.

Truth 2: Love is the essential mark of a Christian

Love is the essential mark of a Christian. Christian love does not mean blanket acceptance of everything that ever occurs in the world. It means that we are motivated by it and seek to demonstrate it in the world by living according to the principles God has established. The characteristics of love should be evident in your life and relationships.

God's View

God created us to give and receive love. The first and greatest commandment is to love God with all our strength, body, mind, and soul. This is a dynamic thought because before we are taught to do anything else we are commanded to reflect the love of God into the earth. He placed it in us, and we must turn around and show it back to him. God created us in His image and likeness. Being born again equips us with the same attributes of God by virtue of the Spirit dwelling in us.

Love heals. It empowers you to be your best, and it has the power to help others be their best. When we love as God loves, it changes things for the better. There are three types of love: "*phileo*," "*eros*," and "*agape*." God's love toward us is agape.

It is unconditional. Agape or unconditional love is not a love of weakness but of strength. It is a love that gives to another not necessarily what is desired but what the recipient needs. In agape love, the giver is the one who responds appropriately to the needs of the recipient. We have twisted it around. Today we think that one who loves gets to make demands upon the recipient. We hear things like "if you loved me, you would...." I'll let you fill in the blank, because depending on your age and stage of life the demands seem to change.

When a person truly operates in agape love, their desire is to satisfy the needs of the recipient with the things that will position them for success. Agape love has as its highest aim not the satisfaction of the giver but the fulfillment of the recipient. Yet the needs satisfied are not self-serving but God honoring. For example, "For you have need of patience after you have done the will of God." God's love toward us is demonstrated by allowing us time to wait between action and expected outcome. Waiting reveals our true attitude. Now walk a little farther here. God, who gives agape love, is always moving in accordance with this plan. Love is purposeful. The purpose of love is to provide an atmosphere that facilitates growth and success.

God's plan for us is to reflect His image and likeness. He desires that we move with correct motives and keep a pure heart before Him. God knows our hearts, motives, and minds, yet we don't always know. We think our motives and minds are pure, but agape love delivers to us exactly what we need to help us prosper in our journey. It brings to us what we need to cause our change, deliverance, and prosperity. God wants us to operate in love the same way He does.

Because we don't always have a clear understanding of what love is and what it is not, we tend to make up rules that we use to guide us in our love relationships. I call these myths because we really think the spiritual world operates according to our thoughts and beliefs.

Renew Your Mind...

Think about the previous chapter. What challenged your thinking in this area? Take a moment and interact with the material by journaling your thoughts prior to reading and your thoughts now.

_____

_____

_____

_____

_____

_____

_____

_____

_____

Transform Your Walk...

Change occurs when we move from thinking to doing. Change involves action. What have your thoughts about pain and difficulties been up to this point? What ideas do you need to let go of in order to have a correct view of pain and suffering and to mature in your spiritual walk?

_____

_____

_____

_____

_____

_____

_____

_____

_____

_____

Chapter Eight

God Didn't Say...
Things Will Never Change

"And the manna ceased on the morrow
after they had eaten of the old corn of the land;
neither had the children of Israel manna any more;
but they did eat of the fruit
of the land of Canaan that year." Joshua 5:12

Setting the Stage

The children of Israel wandered through the wilderness for 40 years and God's supernatural provision kept them clothed and fed. Miraculously their clothes and shoes never wore out. God provided manna and quail when they needed food; and water from a rock to quench their thirst. Manna was God's miraculous provision for the children of Israel, and they ate it for forty years.

After forty years of living in the wilderness and receiving God's provision, the children of Israel probably grew quite comfortable with how God moved; or at least how they expected Him to move. In fact, they were probably so comfortable with the provision God made they took it for granted. As if, things would never change. Believers tend to do the same thing. We get comfortable or familiar with one method God uses in our lives and begin to think things will never change. This was not the case for the children of Israel and it is rarely the case for us. Manna was not the eternal provision for Israel it was given for a specific purpose and a designated timeframe. Eventually, God stopped providing manna for them. Yet manna was not given to the children of Israel just provide then with a source for food for them but also to help them realize God was ultimately their source. Their dependency was to rest solely on God. The method of His provision changed and the children of Israel had to accept the change, adapt to it, and acknowledge God was still their sovereign provider. Their situation is not different than what we experience. God provides for us and we get so comfortable with the way things happen that if His provision ceases in the manner or method we are accustomed too, we panic. Sometimes this panic causes us to buckle under pressure. Many times, we build a entire theological paradigm on the methods when in fact, it is not Gods methods that are most important but His principles. God can and will use a variety of methods to accomplish His will but they all proceed out of established principles. Your expectations should be based on the truth of the principles. God's methods may change but His principles never will.

God's assurance for us is that there will always be provision and that provision will be sufficient for our needs. Herein lies the challenge. Sometimes our comfort with how God makes provision in our lives leaves us ill prepared for change. We forget if only on a subconscious level that God is sovereign and has the authority to change how things happen in our lives. We must be dependent on Him and not stuck on the methods.

God didn't say His things will never change. He says that He doesn't change. In order to flow with God and live a life of greater peace you must be able to handle change effectively. It has been said that the one constant thing in life is change. Change is not arbitrary and can be a prelude to your greatest blessing. However, your thoughts and attitudes about change must be in line with the will of God. Let's address some common thoughts that keep us from triumphantly handling change.

Addressing Spiritual Myths
Myth 1: If it isn't broken don't fix it

A very common thought is that if something is working, there is no need to consider improvement. This tells us that if something is working fine, we should leave it alone. We resist change simply because we cannot see the outcome. It is an established fact that God provides for His children and sometimes miraculously. We must learn to be flexible and allow change to be a part of our experience. Our resistance to change can shut out all that God has promised us. In effect, we can close off the next dimension of moving into our destiny because of our resistance to change.

Myth 2: We've always done it this way

This statement has probably heralded the fall of many organizations, religious and secular. Although we are creatures of habit, pattern, and order this does not mean things must always be done the same way. Living a powerful, faith filled life requires a certain level of openness to innovation and improvements. Improving systems, processes and programs can be the catalyst for greater mission accomplishment. One reason this myth has such power revolves around the thought any attempt to change the status quo somehow makes the old way invalid. If the thought that the old way is now considered to be bad or wrong instead of having served a vital purpose there is a great resistance to change. The fact that this is not the case must be thoroughly explored, whether the change is to occur on a personal or professional level. There must be a common understanding that improvements or changes are made in order to make things easier, simpler, or better for both the producer and the consumer. Change does not have to be considered bad. Change does not mean that the old way was wrong. Change is not a personal statement against people or their ideas. Change is simply an altering of a state to influence or cause a desired result. To conquer this myth, recognize that the words Solomon penned in Ecclesiastes 3:1, "to every thing there is a season and a time to every purpose under heaven" are true. Essentially, it tells us that there are appointed times for everything and that life brings change.

Myth 3: Other people won't like the change

Anytime you resist change because of what others might think, you in essence abdicate your power. You give power to that which is unknown. Speculation and innuendo are not components of spiritual power. Although it is wise to consider the thoughts, feelings, and ideas of others; if their concerns keep you from moving forward with a God inspired idea you have given them a level of power and influence that should be reserved for God. People will not always like or be amenable to change but don't let that stop you from implementing any change that produces forward progress. This myth gains its power because it taps into a personal fear of what others think. It is based on assumption and not the facts of faith. God's word says, "when a man's ways please the Lord, He will make even his enemies be at peace with him" Proverbs 16:7. Thinking of this in the context of change, when the changes you make please God, His acceptance of it will cause people to be at peace with you. Now this doesn't mean that everyone will suddenly like the changes you implement but opposition will be annulled. Never let the assumed reactions of others keep you from change.

Imparting Spiritual Truth
Truth 1: Change will come

Just as the children of Israel came to a place where God stopped providing manna for them; a day will come when manna ceases to exist in your life. You should understand that the cessation of manna is not a cause for alarm but a time to rejoice. It is not a time to resign yourself to giving up and giving in; it is a time to witness and understand that God has something more in store for you. If God made miraculous provision to sustain you, then have confidence that He will continue to make provision for you.

When God stops providing resources one way (i.e. manna) it represents coming to the end of a season. It sends a clear message that you are entering new territory and there is another supply available to you. Manna must stop when you step into a new level of the promise. This truth is demonstrated with Israel it will demonstrated with you. *"And the manna ceased on the morrow after they had eaten of the old corn of the land; neither had the children of Israel manna any more; but they did eat of the fruit of the land of Canaan that year."(Joshua 5:12)* There is no need for manna in the promised land. The land yields it fruits and provides sustenance for your life. In the land of milk and honey, there is no need for manna.

Exodus 16:35 reads, *"The children of Israel did eat manna forty years, **until** they came to a land inhabited; they did eat manna **until** they came unto the borders of the land of Canaan."*

John 6:49 says, *"Your fathers did eat manna in the wilderness, and are dead."* When we are eating manna, we are not in the Promised Land. We must look forward to the cessation of manna. It signals that we have moved out of the wilderness experience into the promise. Never should you be content to simply live on manna the rest of your life. God has other ways of providing for you.

Another example of God changing the method of provision can be seen in the example of the prophet Elijah. When God was preparing him for service, He told him to go to a place, hide himself, and drink from the brook Cherith. God sent ravens to feed him. Elijah obeyed and was sustained, but then it was time for the prophet to move to the next stage of the plan. The brook dried up and God gave new instructions. The Lord stopped one method of provision and introduced another. We see it in 1 Kings 17:9, "A*nd the word of the Lord came unto him saying Arise, get to Zarephath and dwell there, behold I have commanded a widow woman to sustain thee."* When God changed the method of provision, Elijah went with the program. He obeyed. We must learn to follow suit and not resist a move of God in our lives.

Truth 2: Realize that Jesus gives you more than manna

The children of Israel didn't wholeheartedly believe in God, they believed in the provision. They still had issue with God for they still walked in disobedience. They refused to look beyond the miraculous and see the glory that would lead to eternal life. In fact, there will come a day when God's miraculous provision for the wilderness in the way it has been coming will cease.

God does not have one way to provide for your life. We tend to think that if something doesn't happen then we won't be successful, or if we don't get it the way we expected it won't work out. When we pray, we talk to God with our own mindset and expectations, but He answers us according to spiritual truth. We think that if God provided for us one way before, He will do it the same way again. We can be certain that God will provide, but we can never rest with complete certainty that He will do it the same way twice, three times, or forever. He may have done it that way for forty years then decide this way is more profitable this time. In college, a friend of mine managed money poorly. Whenever he obtained some, he would waste it on fast food and other non-essential things. One day, he asked his parents for more money to buy groceries and they responded to his request. The interesting thing here is that they began to send him gift certificates for the grocery store instead of cash for his pocket. He was not excited about the change and complained for a while but then realized he was still getting what he needed. God works the same way in our lives. The change in how God provides may make you feel uncomfortable for a while but ultimately it brings you the experience God needs you to have for your growth, development and victory.

God will ensure the resources you are given are the provision you need. So if you believe you do not have the resources you need to accomplish the task, ask yourself is it really the task or is it the timing?

Truth 3: A change in provision is a sign of hope and renewed blessing

A change in how God makes provision in your life is a sign of hope and assurance. It confirms that He will fulfill His promises to you. Israel ate manna for forty years but, the first day they stepped into the Promised Land manna ceased. The manna was no longer necessary. The Promised Land was full of milk and honey. It contained the provision they needed for survival. When they entered a new location, they could not be tied to old methods. In the wilderness, manna was the representation of God's miraculous provision. God provided manna in the absence of food. It also demonstrated the God was the supplier of their need. In Canaan, manna represented the old way God provided for them. When God stopped producing manna for the children of Israel, it was a clear signal that they entered not just another physical stage but another spiritual stage as well. God's provision is purposeful. It not only provides for your needs but also matures you by providing spiritual knowledge. Initially,

God gave manna in the wilderness in response to their lack of food. His miraculous provision revealed to the Israelites that He was their source. Each day, Israel was to recognize God as their provider. They were to gain confidence and trust in God not in the supply. Likewise, in your spiritual walk, when God provides something for you do not get caught up on the provision itself but stay focused on the provider. Remember that God is working in your life not just to bring you physical comfort but also to bring you to a deeper relationship with Him.

When things change, it is not a time for panic or fear. It is a time to rejoice. The Lord has another plan for you that will continue to move you along your appointed path. When you are in the midst of change and fell a little panicky remember, Proverbs 3:5-6 "Trust in the Lord with all thine heart, lean not unto thine own understanding but in all they ways acknowledge Him and He shall direct your path." Change will touch your life it is inevitable. Whether you have to change how you do something or if God makes provision differently in order to prevail with power you must be willing to accept those changes knowing there are great blessings in store.

God's View

God is never overly concerned with change. He is the author of change. Think about it, seasons change, day changes to night, the Holy Spirit produces change in people. Contrary to what many think, He is not averse to change. God may change the manner in which something is delivered to you or sometimes even the method. It is His sovereign prerogative. What does not change are the principles of God. Consider the children of Israel from their wilderness wandering to Joshua's crossing of the Jordan. In both instances, they had to overcome an obstacle that kept them from their destiny. As the children of Israel left Egypt, they came to a place where Pharaoh's army was pursuing them and God divided the waters that they could walk over on dry ground; but when they needed to cross the Jordan under Joshua's leadership God wanted them to step into the water first. God administered help in a different manner. He never changed His character or His nature. Although the method of their deliverance was different, His principles remained constant: God is a Deliverer, God will make a way, God is your protector, and God can do the impossible.

As you embrace change in your life just remember that God's principles do not change. Embrace the principles and be open to how He wants to bless you.

Renew Your Mind...

Change is inevitable, but when our spiritual journey requires change in the method or manner of provision, we feel uncomfortable. What challenged your thinking in this area? Take a moment and interact with the material by journaling your thoughts prior to reading and your thoughts now.

_____

_____

_____

_____

_____

_____

_____

_____

_____

Transform Your Walk...

Change is inevitable. It will touch your life. Can you see evidence of God's change in provision in your life? How did you feel? Were you quick to adjust to the change or was it challenging? In light of your new thinking about change, how will you react now?

_____

_____

_____

_____

_____

_____

_____

_____

_____

Chapter Nine

God Didn't Say...
Forgive If You Feel Like It

"But if ye forgive not men their trespasses,
neither will your Father forgive your trespasses."
Matthew 6:15

Setting the Stage

Let us face it—we have all experienced hurt feelings, wounded emotions, and maybe even physical pain because of someone else's behavior. The effects of these experiences may have caused the break down of a relationship, damaged your self-esteem, or maybe even worse. The truth is, life is not always pretty and things do happen; but do not under estimate the importance of forgiveness and the power it releases into your life.

When we were children and a friend did something to us, we felt compelled to forgive. We usually forgave them and made amends. When someone that we were not friends with did something to us, we usually chose not to forgive them. Occasionally, we might set up a series of things they had to do before we would forgive. It seemed like fun and games but it created in us a method of instituting our own standards of forgiveness. In essence, we developed a "forgiveness meter." This meter collected data like: who, what, when, where, why, and how. It also registered pain, embarrassment, and offensiveness of the incident. Depending on where the meter registered the offense, we determined how soon we could forgive and mend the relationship or whether we could forgive at all. From this, we developed a belief that forgiveness was optional and that our standard of judgment was correct. The challenge here is that only part of that statement is true. God has given us power to forgive, but His standard is more righteous ours. Forgiveness is necessary, and it opens the door to kingdom expansion and unity in the body of Christ. The standard is God's: doing for others as we would have done to us. The interesting thing to note is that forgiveness has greater spiritual significance than ever imagined. In order to renew our minds we must be willing to destroy faulty thinking about forgiveness and walk in obedience to the Word of God.

Many times our subconscious thoughts about an issue are often the sticking point, the point that keeps us glued to the past instead of walking triumphantly into the future. It is time to move beyond fears and myths to a life where we experience the spiritual power that comes from forgiveness. Though the work may be a little challenging, the results are worth it. Dig in.

Addressing Spiritual Myths
Myth 1: To forgive means to accept what has been done
Many times, we don't want to forgive because it feels like we're saying that what occurred was okay. This is scary, especially when dealing with issues that register high on the heinous acts meter. We usually feel the only thing we can do is hold unforgiveness to maintain a sense of control over the situation. Ironically, the attempt to maintain control usually becomes a prison and not the place of freedom one would

expect. Energy is expended in holding unforgiveness. You are not free to hold onto other things. You must face the fear of letting go and address it directly.

Myth 2: I can forgive some things but not others
Here we typically paint ourselves into a corner when we decide which sin should be forgiven and which should not. We are in essence saying there is greater weight for me than for another. Romans 3:23 tells us, *"For the wages of sin is death, but the gift of God is eternal life...."* When looking at sin from God's point of view you find there is no "little one" vs. "big one" measuring stick. Sin is sin and the penalty for all of it is death. When we ascribe value to sins committed against us, we stand outside the biblical definition of protocol given to us from the Holy Spirit.

Myth 3: Forgiveness is a process
What really happens here is we give ourselves permission not to forgive. By telling ourselves it is a process, we are agreeing by default to set up a standard of time not to forgive. Forgiveness is a decision not an emotion. It is debt release, pure and simple. If you hold someone partially responsible for the debt then it has not been forgiven.

Imparting Spiritual Truth
Forgiveness does not mean acceptance of what happened. To forgive someone does not dismiss the act or subsequent consequences. It is only a cancellation of debt. When someone does something to us, we believe they owe us something and that is why we get hurt or offended. For example, when a person goes outside of marriage and commits adultery, the faithful spouse feels victimized and has difficulty forgiving. The offended spouse probably has a lot of feelings—anger, hurt, shock, amazement, etc. Yet when you look at the heart of the issue, you find that once they get past the emotional

reactions is only the beginning. It is here that facing the prospect of forgiving becomes difficult if your thoughts are not undergirded by the Word of God. Essentially, the work of forgiveness begins with an examination of broken expectations not focusing on the act itself. Identifying what was expected, and then releasing one from that debt. The offended spouse then has the challenge of letting go of the debt and moving forward or staying stuck. More specifically, when you believe someone owes you love and they did not give it to you, you must recognize that and make a decision to forgive. It is not simply about an improper action. (Let me include a caveat here. I am not making any statements on marriage or relationships only the proper application of forgiveness in the life of a believer.)

I can recall a session with a client in which a discussion on forgiveness arose. When asked if they had forgiven the person who hurt them, they said, "Oh yes, I did that a long time ago." Then without any hesitation they said, "I'll just be glad when they're dead." That was a powerful statement. It revealed the truth about their heart. I had to stop them and ask, "So you still require them to pay for what they did with their life?" It made the client stop and think. I hope it makes you stop and think too. Forgiveness means releasing someone from the debt they owe you. Our hearts and minds sometimes conspire to make us think we have forgiven when in actuality if we require anything of the person, from an apology to a thank you to their lives, then we stand in the place of unforgiveness. The fact that forgiveness is necessary supports the theory that a debt was incurred. Forgiveness therefore becomes a choice, a deliberate decision. The choice springs out of the reality that the person that offended or caused harm to you could never repay the debt. It has little to do with them being sorry, apologetic or contrite. Forgiveness is based on the truth that what is owed is more than what can be given. There are examples of this throughout the Bible but we have to look no further than God's forgiveness of us. God forgives us our sin. Jesus paid what was owed as the result of our sin. We have no capacity to pay even though at some point in our lives we may become aware of the debt. If not for the grace and forgiveness of God, we would not be able to enter into a proper relationship. Although we may want to repay we lack the capacity to do so. Subsequently, the one who offers forgiveness acknowledges that the debt is beyond what the person can pay and subsequently releases the other person from it.

Forgiveness is not just an arbitrary idea springing from the mind of God; the spiritual ramifications are huge. Your act of forgiveness clears the path for God to move in the life of the offender and the offended (you). Your act of forgiveness frees the offender. Often you must remember that God has forgiven you of your sin, a debt you could not pay, and now you have an opportunity to do the same thing for someone else. They literally could not give what was required at the time; if they could have they would not have offended you. If you keep that thought in mind it becomes easier to understand the concept of forgiveness. Forgiveness is erasing a debt. Your act of forgiveness helps the offender see God. It opens up the way for the operation of the Holy Spirit. It is such an important concept. If we do not forgive then how can the world believe that God, who is unseen, will forgive their sin? Forgiveness paves the way for kingdom expansion.

Matthew 3:3 declares, *"Prepare ye the way of the Lord, make his paths straight."* God travels down roads of righteousness. This doesn't mean things won't come into the road that aren't righteous, but as we pave a road with forgiveness we actually open a path for the Spirit of God to travel down. When God starts moving, everything in His path will be dealt with. His desire is to have access to man. Our proper use of forgiveness can pave the way for the Lord to move.

The freedom found in forgiveness is twofold. Number one, you recognize that any situation void of God will never be able to meet the requirements you have. The truth is we all have needs—the need to be loved, respected, accepted, purposeful, etc. Each day we seek to get those needs met. Often we place the responsibility of meeting those needs on others, and when they fail to meet them we hold them accountable. As forgiveness becomes an intrinsic part of who we are, we begin to recognize that God is the supplier of all our need. Forgiveness is an important part of getting the world onto God's big picture. Understanding the concept from God's perspective helps you become a willing forgiver.

The inability to forgive others makes it difficult for them to see or believe that God can and will forgive their sins. How can one believe that God, who is unseen, will forgive their sins when God's representative, who is seen, is not able to do so? Looking at it from that perspective drives home the point that our forgiveness or lack thereof can be the crux of someone's salvation. That's a huge shift in perspective. Forgiveness has always been thought of as being about the person who suffered the hurt, pain, or disappointment, but we should now be able to see that the one who caused offense is desperately in need as well.

Matthew 18:6-7 says, *"But whoso shall offend one of these little ones which believe in me, it were better for him that a millstone were hanged about his neck, and that he were drowned in the depth of the sea. Woe unto the world because of offences! for it must needs be that offences come; but woe to that man by whom the offence cometh!"* Offenses are not shocking to God; He knows they will happen. He has already made provision for them. Through these particular scriptures we also see that it is not even necessary to fight. God is already on the case, taking care of you when you are offended.

Remember Peter's words to Jesus: "How many times shall I forgive my brother if he sins against me? Seven?"

to which Jesus responded, "Not seven but seventy times seven." Jesus knew the disciples didn't get it. Forgiveness is not about your feelings being hurt, it's about debt plain and simple. However, beyond the understanding of forgiveness as debt cancellation, we must also recognize there is a great admiration attached to forgiveness. Matthew 6:14-15 says, *"For if ye forgive men their trespasses, your heavenly Father will also forgive you: but if ye forgive not men their trespasses, neither will your Father forgive your trespasses."* And Matthew 18:35: *"So likewise shall my heavenly Father do also unto you, if ye from your hearts forgive not every one his brother their trespasses."*

The admonition from God is that forgiveness of our trespasses is contingent upon our ability to forgive. It is tied to our salvation. If we have no faith in God's power, authority, and provision in our lives, then we lack the faith to believe He could forgive us our debts. If we lack the faith to believe He could forgive us our debts and cancel all payments due, then we haven't truly received salvation. Salvation is receiving Jesus' death for the payment of our sin; it is God's free gift to us. Our ability and willingness to forgive is squarely set upon our belief that God has forgiven us. When we receive grace, we become givers of grace.

Don't panic though. Forgiveness does not mean we have to like or accept what was done. It also doesn't mean that consequences are not in order. Recall from the chapter on consequences that all actions initiate a series of consequences. You cannot stop a consequence; you can only gain God's strength, protection, and mercy to ensure it doesn't harm you. When we offer forgiveness, the door to kingdom expansion is opened. When a person offends you and asks for forgiveness, they are on some level aware that a problem was caused. It is this awareness that can give way to godly sorrow. 2 Corinthians 7:10 says, *"For the godly sorrow worketh repentance to salvation not to be repented of: but the sorrow of the world worketh death."* Godly sorrow is the recognition of Gods perspective that causes one to reconsider their way of thinking of behaving. When one sees a situation from Gods point of view it lead to repentance. Repentance is an inward change of mind that produces an outward change in actions. Therefore, a person actually begins to embrace the mind of God, which reforms their actions. Repentance to salvation is a change of mind that produces deliverance from a material or temporary situation.

Truth 1: Forgiveness is a deliberate choice

Debt release is an act. Forgiveness is debt release. It is not a process. There is no partial forgiveness. It is all or nothing. God does not partially forgive you of your sin. He forgives all your sin. We must follow in the path He has paved for us.

Truth 2: Forgiveness does not negate wrongdoing or consequences

Sometimes challenges arise with forgiveness because on a very human level we think it means ignoring the seriousness or the pain caused by the act. Forgiving someone does not diminish the seriousness of the incident; it simply releases them from the debt they owe.

Truth 3: Forgiveness glorifies God

When you fully grasp the concept of forgiveness, you become aware that when you forgive others you are operating in the image of God. God has forgiven you substantial sin, sin that had a cost and that cost is your life. Yet He chose to die for your sin. What an awesome price Jesus paid! You never could have paid that debt. When it comes to forgiving others, you must remember that your debt has been erased. It glorifies God because you are reflecting all that He is in the earth.

God's View

It is hard to miss the importance of forgiveness in the mind of God. After all, it is through forgiveness of sin that we are able to receive the gift of salvation. God expects those, who have received the ultimate in forgiveness, to recognize its value and freely offer it to others. To be able to forgive is to have complete faith in and respect for what God's forgiveness has done for you. It requires confidence that He is the supplier all your needs. Your ability to forgive does not mean that your were not hurt or did not have a need. It does diminish your value or worth. It simply indicates that you trust God to supply all of your needs not another individual. You trust Him so completely that you can release others from debt they do not have the capacity to pay. You do not hold a debt against someone that cannot pay in order to feel better. Forgiveness clearly demonstrates that you even trust God so much that He can send the supply through another source. For example, when someone offends you because they did not give you love or respect. Your decision to forgive them doesn't mean you don't need love or respect it simply means that their inability to give it to you will not keep you bound or unable to move forward. The forgiver recognizes the sovereign ability of God to supply all their needs through a variety of methods.

Forgiveness is given from a place of abundance, not lack. When you are able to release someone from debt, it is because you recognize you do not really need what is owed to survive. In Mathew 18:21-35, Jesus outlined the importance of forgiveness. The parable states that a man owed money to the king. It was a lot of money. He was not able to pay it. He asked for mercy and the king forgave the debt. The king was able to forgive the debt because he was the king, and his authority, power, and wealth did not rest on what someone else owed. You must understand this concept. Your identity is not based on the ability of others to give to you but rests in the word of God. You stand in a position of authority, influence and power, because God has established your identity through His word. You are the child of the King. You are fearfully and wonderfully made. You are more than a conqueror. When you are confident in the power you have you realize that you can forgive others who do not honor that because it is their deficiency not yours. If you only feel loved, appreciated, or worthy based on what someone else gives you, then you operate from a sense of lack and not abundance. Conversely, if someone's doing something to you takes away all that you are, you never really had as much as you thought you did to begin with. God says we are able to forgive because He supplies all our needs.

When our view mirrors God's view, we receive the gift of forgiveness and all the benefits that come with it. We find that we are far wealthier than we ever could have imagined. Offenses don't deplete us; they remind us of what God supplies and the needs of others.

God desires that we think beyond ourselves, that we look beyond their fault, see their need, and respond appropriately. You should always extend the life preserver of forgiveness, recognizing that your ability to do so may be the absolute best chance for someone to experience the truth salvation. Forgive always and pray without ceasing, because God didn't say that forgiveness is based on how you feel about the situation.

Renew Your Mind...

Forgiveness is an act. What challenged your thinking in this area? Take a moment and interact with the material by journaling your thoughts prior to reading and your thoughts now.

_____

_____

_____

_____

_____

_____

_____

_____

Transform Your Walk...

Forgiveness opens the door to great and beautiful blessings. Sometimes those doors are closed because we simply have not forgiven ourselves for past actions or decisions. Today decide to agree with God and forgive yourself of things that may have been contrary to His will. Then make a list of people you feel still owe you a debt and decide to forgive them wholeheartedly. You may feel it is enough to do this internally, or you may want to call them and show forth the love of Christ.

_____

_____

_____

_____

_____

_____

_____

_____

Chapter Ten

God Didn't Say...
Trust Is the Same as Belief

*"Commit thy way unto the Lord; trust also in him;
and he shall bring it to pass" Psalm 37:5*

Setting the Stage

Christiana was a young woman who desperately wanted a child. Each month she would wait with anticipation for a positive pregnancy test but each month she was disappointed. For two years, Christiana and her husband endured monthly heartbreaks, as their dreams of conception seem to fade away. They were certain it was the will of God for them to have a child of their own. They believed. Yet after another heartbreaking year, they began to doubt, and that doubt affected their faith. During one of our conversations, I asked them, "Do you trust God's word?" Christiana responded, "Yes, I believe that it is God's will for me to have a baby." I looked at them and said, "I didn't say believe, I said trust. Trust is not the same as belief. Although we tend to categorize them under the same banner, they are different." When you believe God that is good, faith is what pleases Him but beyond faith, there must be trust. You must trust His word, His ability, and His timing. You must continue to trust regardless of circumstances, situations, or timing. Trust is an attitude. It gives you security and peace. When you trust God, you are secure and carefree, knowing that what He says will happen. You must connect trust and belief in order to live a powerful Christian life. One enemy to the trust-belief connection is anticipation. Anticipation can be relatively innocuous if you are able to keep perspective and not take matters of accomplishing the will of God in your own hands but anticipation can also become the beginning of creating a series of uninspired events. When anticipation takes on a life of its own it links up with personal desires and develops its own timetable and schedule for the promise to be realized.

Abraham and Sarah, received a very similar word from God, they would have a child. They believed but they did not trust. They believed and they wanted a child. Their belief combined with their desire produced a perverse anticipation. This anticipation of the promise caused them to take matters in their own hands and Abraham became the father of Ishmael. Sometimes our desires mixed with anticipation causes us to forget about the sovereignty of God and His perfect plan for our lives. Sometimes anticipation causes us to move ahead of the plan of God. Their anticipation causes a lot of trouble in their lives. The same can happen or perhaps has already happened in your life. Abraham and Sarah believed but did not trust enough to stand on the Word. Throughout their lives, they learned the valuable lessons of trust. They learned these lessons well. So great were these lessons that when God required Isaac, their only son to be sacrificed Abraham moved in obedience because he trusted in the Word of God. We, too, must learn to trust and rely on Him regardless of circumstances. First, though we must learn to identify when we are moving with a lack of trust by addressing some common beliefs that break the belief-trust connection.

Addressing Spiritual Myths

Myth 1: If I have faith, then I automatically trust God

This is easy to believe and most people do but this myth ignores the true meaning of faith. To have faith is to believe, to be persuaded, or have confidence in the truth of a person or idea. To trust is to rely on the character, strength, or truth of someone. When you have faith, you believe that God is true. When you have trust, you rely on His ability to make His word good. Faith does not automatically give rise to trust. Trust is only demonstrated when one must rely on something to become true. A bungee jumper must trust in the cord that secures him. A paratrooper must trust in the parachute that will open and help him land. The bungee jumper believes in the safety of the sport but he must trust the cord. The paratrooper believes in the ability of the parachute but he must trust that it will work every time he jumps out of a plane. Likewise, we believe that God is our God. We must trust that He is able to do all that He says, in spite of what things look like to our natural eye. Faith obligates us to move to the realm of trust. It is not automatic but it is a decision. Trust is a decision. Thinking that faith automatically brings trust causes us to assume we do not have any further duties or responsibilities toward God. This is not true, because when faith is present there must also be a continuation of trust. Trust does not just happen. Trust is given, and the proper management of trust brings more trust. Our responsibility is to give or extend our trust to God by seeking help and refuge from Him.

Myth 2: Trust is the same as belief

Just to reiterate the point, faith believes in something while trust is having confidence in it. Trust is relying on something, and it follows belief. You must recognize that trust is not the same as belief. If you continue to believe this myth, your walk of faith will not take the proper shape.

Trust produces confidence and security, and reduces anxiety. Belief without trust might give you insight about the plan of God but leaves you void of the endurance through the process. Belief without trust causes you to feel the need to make things happen. When you have believed God and not trusted Him you will still feel a need to make things happen. You might hear the word or understand the will of God but miss the process and plan. Proverbs 3:5, *"Trust in the Lord with all thine heart; and lean not unto thine own understanding"* tells us to trust in the Lord with all our heart. Trust is a heart issue.

Myth 3: Trust is automatic

Trust is not automatic. Trust is extended based on the fidelity of the one making a statement or request. When you extend your trust to someone, you are relying on his or her character and past performance. They have proven, at least on some level they are trustworthy. When they continue to present evidence that they can be relied upon you extend more trust. It creates a cycle. You rely on them, they prove they can be relied upon, and you rely on them more. Now relate this concept to your relationship with God. You build trust the same way. God says something and you believe it. You rely on it. It happens. You now know God's word is true. You trust Him more. You obey more. Trust is not automatic.

The Issue of Unbelief

Nothing is more important to God than our belief. It is our belief in the work of Jesus Christ that saves and sanctifies us. Our belief positions us to love and worship Him. Trust enlarges the concept because it brings our belief to the point of action. James 2:19 records, *"Thou believest that there is one God; thou doest well: the devils also believe, and tremble."* When we think all we have to do is say we believe in God and all is right in the world we do not exist beyond the level of devils.

What separates a believer from the level of the devils who also believe is the ability of our belief to produce action that corresponds to the word. When we believe in God and trust in His word, our actions should demonstrate it. Trusting God causes you to be victorious through the most difficult processes.

The journey to the cross had many steps and each one required a new level of trust and humility. Each one had to be handled meticulously for redemption to take place. Jesus had to completely trust in the process that was laid before him. If he did not rely on the process the Father had established, he (at least theoretically) could have decided on a different plan to make it happen. Trusting God to carry you through the processes of your life is just as important. You believe that He has spoken a word concerning your life now you must trust Him through the process. Trusting God through the processes of your life becomes easier as you identify the main obstacle to that trust. The main obstacle to trust is unbelief.

Brace yourselves: everyone must address unbelief in his or her life. You must not only acknowledge but also repent of revealed unbelief in your life. This causes powerful spiritual renewal and transformation.

In each of the Gospels, Jesus repeatedly addressed the issue of unbelief. He used various scenarios, parable, and examples to deal with eliminating unbelief. He practically demonstrated the fact that belief must be paired with trust in order to accomplish its highest aim. On several occasions, he revealed that unbelief would render them powerless. Furthermore, He showed that faith was necessary in the lives of those He helped by assessing their level of faith. The account of Jesus restoring the sight of the blind men in the gospel of Matthew, gives a clear example of His constant assessment of belief. *"And when he was come into the house, the blind men came to him: and Jesus saith unto them, Believe ye that I am able to do this? They said unto him, Yea Lord."* *(Matthew 9:28)* Jesus demonstrated the necessity of faith. He is our example of the proper way to live and work on Earth as we relate to God the Father. Jesus' attention to the connection between trust and belief should spark a desire in us to understand the power of trust and belief in our own lives. Our understanding of this powerful union should be evidenced in our behavior, yet sometimes we miss the lessons God is teaching. We can find ourselves in the right place, at the right time, doing the right things and still miss the lesson God is teaching. Thankfully, though, God will always work on our behalf to help us believe.

John 11 gives us a beautiful example of all the dynamic elements of the belief-trust connection. This connection produces supernatural occurrence in your life.

The account of the Lazarus' resurrection can help us understand some of the nuances of this connection. The disciples were with Jesus, right place, right time, doing the right thing. Jesus demonstrated how trusting God would not only increase their belief but also keep them moving according to the Spirit. Trusting God, relying on His guidance will cause you to obey Him completely. When you rely on Him, you will allow Him to determine the timing of your life. You will not be in a rush to accomplish something because of emotional attachment. You will be confident of His timing and His ability. Jesus demonstrated that for the disciples in this incident but they did not get it. When He received the news that Lazarus was sick, he made a powerful statement, *"this sickness is not unto death, but for the glory of God, that the Son of God might be glorified"* John 11:4. Then He remained two days longer even though He loved Mary, Martha, and Lazarus. This is a clear demonstration of trust in God superseding emotion. He goes on to say to them, metaphorically, *"Our friend Lazarus sleepeth; but I go, that I may awake him out of sleep."* Their answer, *"Lord, if he is sleeping he shall do well" John 11:11-12*, reveals the fact that they still did not fully comprehend what was happening. God was taking them to another level of belief. Jesus revealed great truth to them and they missed it. He revealed some of the glory and they missed it. How often does God reveal something awesome to us and we miss it?

Jesus knew a communication failure had occurred and said, *"...Lazarus is dead. "And I am glad for your sakes that I was not there, to the intent ye may believe; nevertheless let us go unto him." John 11:14-15*. Jesus revealed the events that would transpire would lead to an increase in their belief. We must realize that events in our life increase our belief, which leads us to greater trust. Spiritual reformation comes when we allow the Holy Sprit to work within us.

One of the greatest obstacles in the life of a believer is unbelief. Have you ever stopped to think about what you really believe and where those thoughts come from? Why do I believe what I believe? Do I really believe what I *think* I do?

Imparting Spiritual Truth
Truth 1: Belief and trust bring the fulfillment of the promises of God

Hebrews 3:19 reminds us that the children of Israel could not enter into rest because of their unbelief. Numbers 14 tells us they could not enter the Promised Land because of unbelief. If unbelief keeps you out then belief must be the key to entering. Belief causes you to walk in all the blessings of God. Paul says, in Romans 4:3 *"Abraham believed God and it was imputed to him as righteousness."* Abraham believed that God would fulfill His promises to Him. After a few missteps, he learned to trust God completely. We too, must learn to trust God through process. We can rely on Him regardless of what a situation looks like, knowing that

God can do the impossible. The fulfillment of the promises God has made to you are only waiting for your belief-trust connection to be in complete operation.

Truth 2: Belief and trust releases the power of God
Matthew 13:58 says, *"...and did not many mighty works there because of their unbelief."* Unbelief hindered the work of Jesus. In His own town, He was not able to release the power of God to save, heal, and deliver at the level that His heart desired because the people did not believe. If unbelief kept Jesus from doing all He desired, what can it do in your life? Belief releases the power of God to work in your life. It is not just something you give out, but it first penetrates you. Luke 10:19 says that Jesus told the Twelve, *"Behold I give unto you power to tread on serpents and scorpions and nothing shall by any means hurt you."* Belief takes away fear. Belief cancels out confusion. Belief interrupts shame and guilt. Belief does a great work in you. Belief gives you greater power. Trust causes you to act on what you believe which releases the power of God.

Truth 3: Belief and trust increase your passion for God
Jesus was passionate about doing God's will no matter what it cost. He said, "My meat is to do the will of the Father." Belief helps us to understand how you should act. Belief gives you life focus but connected to trust, it helps you properly prioritize the actions and activities of your life. Trust gives you the assurance to move into action. Trust causes you to make deliberate choices to live by God's word. When you rely on God, you are really relying on the Word He has spoken and that causes you to decide to obey it. It is really the only way that you will know that God's word has power. It guides the decisions that you make. In fact, it makes decision making a little easier. Belief and trust move you along your divine path. Belief gives you vision and trust gives you an

action plan. The combination of trust and belief move gives you more experience with the reliability of His word. When you realize His word will never fail it causes you extend more trust. This means you are willing to trust and obey more of the Word. This increases your passion for Him.

God's View

Many times, we think that belief in God is enough but there is more. There are other elements that connect to belief that must be understood: love, faith, and trust. Christianity is not a practice of mind over matter. It is not an attempt to psyche your self into believing something. However, many Christians inadvertently fall into this practice by thinking all they have to do is think about something hard enough and it will be sufficient. They try to psych themselves into thinking they believe instead of really addressing their unbelief. When you begin to think of your life and actions ask this question, "What is it that I do not believe about God's word concerning this? If you find that you believe the word, the next move is to extend trust. If you *think* you believe the word but are unable to obey it, unbelief is present. You must address it. Everything you do is connected to what you believe. You only do what you believe. For example, if you are kind to others, then you believe that kindness is important. You might also believe that you should treat others the way you want to be treated. You might also believe that love is kind. You probably also believe that God is Love. Of course, there are less altruistic reasons for being kind but for the purposes of developing a more powerful Christian walk we will stick to those. If you obey, you probably believe there are rewards for obedience, but if you do not obey then you do not believe. You think either there will be no consequences or that they will not be harmful to you.

Unbelief can keep you from seeing the glory of God. It won't keep you from seeing the miracle, but it will keep you from seeing the attributes of God. When you can't identify God's attributes in something, you have truly missed the mark.

What do you believe? Do you believe that Jesus is the resurrection? Do you believe that He is the Truth, the Way, and the Life? Do you believe He is the Prince of Peace? Do you believe that He is the Son of God? That He died for our sins? Do you believe that He has been given all power and authority? Do you believe He can forgive your sins? Do you believe He can restore you? Now think about this, does your life clearly reflect all that you believe?

Be honest with yourself and with God; address areas of unbelief in your life and prepare to move forward. Perhaps your prayer of confession should be, "I have lived with some unbelief. I have been in Your presence. I have seen the miracles. I know who You are. I have been walking with You and talking with You, yet I am ready to go to another level of belief, which always produces a change in action. I am ready. Lord, I believe…"

Renew Your Mind...

Think about the previous chapter. What challenged your thinking in this area? Take a moment and interact with the material by journaling your thoughts prior to reading and your thoughts now.

_____
_____
_____
_____
_____
_____
_____
_____
_____

Transform Your Walk...

Change occurs when we move from thinking to doing. Change involves action. What unbelief has been a part of your Christian experience? Take some time to write them down and then write God's truth about the matter. Allow that truth to shape your thinking.

_____
_____
_____
_____
_____
_____
_____
_____
_____
_____
_____

Chapter Eleven

God Didn't Say...
Do It All by Yourself

"And he gave some apostles; and some, prophets;
and some evangelists; and some, pastors and teachers;
for the perfecting of the saints, for the work of the ministry,
for the edifying of the body of Christ: till we all come in the
unity of the faith, and of the knowledge of the Son of God,
unto a perfect man, unto the measure of the stature
of the fullness of Christ."
Ephesians 4:11-12

Setting the Stage

In the 1940s and '50s there was a radio show that later became a TV show entitled *The Lone Ranger*. The basic premise of the show was that one masked Ranger rode through the plains of Texas administering justice for those who had been wronged. He was the Lone Ranger because, as the history of the story goes (or at least the theme song), the other rangers had been killed in an ambush. The irony is that even the Lone Ranger had help. He relied on the assistance of his friend Tonto and his horse, Silver. "God didn't say do it all by yourself" is the focus of this chapter, and in it the power of unity will be revealed.

One of the greatest lessons I've learned as a leader is that you don't have to do it all, or do it all by yourself. Growing up as what Dr. Kevin Leman of the *Birth Order Book* would call a first born, only child. According to Dr. Leman, I fall into this category because the years between my sibling and me are quite substantial. At any rate, I learned to be self-contained and independent, which to some extent is not bad. However, as I moved into leadership roles with increasing responsibilities, I learned that being too independent has its drawbacks. It was through many leadership experiences, good and bad that the Holy Spirit began to temper my independent nature. The net result of experiences and the work of the Holy Spirit was the realization that "God Didn't Say Do It All by Yourself." It is not necessary to be the Lone Ranger. Everybody has a purpose and our purposes are not independent assets but connectable pieces of Gods bigger plan. Connection brings improved results. Going it alone can diminish your effectiveness and your impact. Connection and unity is evidenced in the Bible from Genesis to Revelation. Even Jesus taught the benefits of connection and not working alone. He declared to the disciples that they would be able to accomplish more when they were connected to the Holy Spirit. He taught and demonstrated the power of connection. He demonstrated it through His connection to the Father; to our connection with Him; and even by outlining the necessity of our connection to others. Jesus helps understand the work of kingdom expansion is not limited to one man. There must be connectivity. Believers must become masters of connectivity. Connection is what expands the kingdom. Connection gives life to vision. Connection increases provision.

The power of connectivity and teamwork are essential to greater success. In John 15, the imagery of Jesus and the vine alludes to our need to be connected for survival.

Ultimately our roots should be in Him, but it is important to be connected to others who are in Him. Jesus sent the disciples out in twos. He even split up the gifts and the work on earth so that we should work together to bring others to maturity and purpose. Jesus states that He is the vine and we are the branches, and apart from Him we can do nothing. God himself reinforces the power and necessity of connections.

Society is not oblivious to this concept; many people are interested in making connections. You can look at the proliferation of social media to support that fact. Our desire to make connections can be seen in professional memberships, organization, and so forth. As a believer, you may want to understand that with everything there is a bigger plan. In today's society many place great value on connections merely for social gain but believers must also have an eye toward the greatest value of connection—the expansion of the reign and authority of God. Many people view making connections as a means to forward their agenda, often with little or no thought to the kingdom agenda. A powerful, faith-filled life is concerned with the kingdom agenda. Although this fact might be known in our subconscious, it is not always played out in daily experience. Living a life of radical faith brings the kingdom agenda to the level of your consciousness. It causes you to think and act differently with regard to connecting to others.

Though some have understood the value of connections, the Lone Ranger attitude is still an insidious issue. God didn't say be the Lone Ranger. This type of attitude keeps people from connecting and serving in churches. Sometimes they hide under the banner of being shy, and sometimes they don't understand that every person's gifts, skills, and abilities are needed for kingdom expansion. Connecting is important. It can increase the effectiveness of your gift. What you are uniquely created to bring to the team is indispensable. By connecting with others who have like faith and are kingdom-minded, you release the power of unity and that brings glory to God. Growth as a Christian happens as you make powerful connections that showcase the beauty and power of unity. Being committed to God's purpose, it becomes evident that our individual purposes are connected.

John 15 beautifully illustrates the power and benefits of connectivity as well as the hazards of being disconnected. Jesus is the true vine, the Father is the husbandman, and we are the branches. Each one connected to the other and each one a vital part of a life-giving plan. Each one supplies a necessary ingredient for a powerful faith filled walk. The benefits of connectivity are seen in the manifestation of power, purpose, and productivity.

Benefits

Power— is the ability to do or act. All power belongs to God and our connection to Him is what gives us true power. When you are connected to God, you have life, not just biological life but spiritual life. True spiritual life is the presence of the Spirit of God within you leading you to all truth and righteousness. True spiritual life proceeds from God and brings to the knowledge of Him, His plan, and your purpose in it. Those who possess true spiritual life are more than merely self-conscious, they are God conscious. They have power not to only promote their personal agenda but to influence the promotion of the kingdom agenda.

Purpose—is the reason something exists. When you are connected to others and work in concert with them, purpose becomes evident. On a personal level, your strengths are high-lighted and your weaknesses covered. Not only does your purpose become evident but also God's purpose becomes evident. Discovering purpose happens in the context of connections. One of the clearest ways to give meaning to your purpose is to connect with others.

Productivity— is the bringing about of abundant or effective results. When you are connected, not only will you fulfill purpose, but you will also bring about an abundance of effective results. Working together helps to accomplish goals faster and easier than one man or woman can going it alone.

Hazards

Separation— to become disconnected. Being separated can cause many issues, but John hits the nail on the head when he declares that apart from Jesus we can do nothing. Separation is the perfect breeding ground for deception. One example I often use is this: the person who sits at home alone every day, reading studying, and praying. In their minds, they are very devout, pious, and loving. Which may be true but piety, devotion and loved is only proven in the service of others. It is easy to believe you love everyone when you stand alone. Connections help reveal truth.

Death—spiritually speaking it is separation from God. Spiritual death occurs when one is not connected to the giver of life. Again, gleaning from the example of vine and branches, if the vine is separated it will eventually wither and die. Similarly, in the life of a believer separation produces death.

Addressing Spiritual Myths

Again, connecting is essential to spiritual growth. It causes you to make full proof of your gifts and experience a richer, more fulfilling life. The concept of connecting with others is equally important in the life of leaders and followers. The effectiveness of your life really can be gauged by your ability or inability to connect with others. In order to release the power found in connection let's address some common myths that cause breakdowns in this area.

Myth 1: I should do it myself if I want it done right

Many people feel they are the best ones to do things and no one else can do them quite the same. To a certain extent, I agree: most people are not going to do something exactly as you would, but does that make their way wrong? For example, a few years ago I worked with a client who was petrified about leaving her daughter with her husband. Her concern was that he would not do the right thing—the right thing being things done exactly as she would do them. Instead of allowing him to help her, she did everything. I really mean everything, which left her exhausted, frustrated and not enjoying life. Interestingly enough, she wanted to be have more time for herself and a better distribution of childcare responsibilities with her husband. One day, I asked her to be specific about what she thought he would do wrong. She began to mention things like picking out clothing, hair bows, eating the wrong foods, etc. I asked her, "What would happen to them (her husband and daughter) if any or all of those things occurred? She replied, "Probably nothing serious." I followed up by asking, if her husband were doing some of those things, what would that allow her to do. She began to outline how she could use the free time. I asked, "So nothing would happen that you consider to be horrible, life-threatening, dangerous, ethically or morally wrong?" She said, "No." I reminded her over all goal of wanting more help. It became clear that she would need to let him help. Through our conversations, it became clear that the phrase "I want it done right" was simply being used as shield for wanting it done her way. In this instance, "right" was subjective. There were no moral or safety considerations but merely a difference in style or manner. As a believer pursuing a more powerful life, you too must recognize when you have not allowed others to help you. Is it because you are living by a subjective notion of what is "right?"

Thinking like this will only cause you to keep too many things on your plate. Believing this myth can cause frustration, excessive tiredness, and burnout.

Myth 2: I am the only one who understands what is important here

This myth will lead you to a life of isolation. Many times we feel, as Elijah did, that we are the only ones left. Our cry is that we can't connect because no one understands or cares about the issue as much as we do. This myth is perpetuated when we fail to see that God has many who are committed to the same purpose and plan. When we think we are the only ones, it feels as if the weight of the world is on our shoulders. This can lead to depression and an inability to make powerful connections to advance the work of the kingdom.

Myth 3: I don't need to connect to others to live a holy life

This is perhaps one of the biggest myths about connecting of all time. A believer who feels they don't need to connect with others or a church is sadly mistaken. It is impossible to grow and flourish in the gifts and graces of God without interaction and connectivity. It is easy to believe you are loving, caring, and compassionate when those traits are never tested by connecting to others. God has not made us to sit in ivory towers but to go forth and be fruitful, multiply, and replenish the earth. When we believe this myth and feel we don't need the body of Christ or others, we are succumbing to a spirit of idolatry, putting ourselves ahead of what God desires for us.

Imparting Spiritual Truth

It is God's desire that we stay connected to one another. He has given each of us different spiritual gifts, skills, and talents. Our differences in perspective and influence enhance the expansion of the kingdom. As long as we are together on the most important fact, that Jesus Christ is Lord of all and the Savior of the world, we can work together to spread the message and influence of the kingdom. Paul talks about connectivity in Philippians 3. Getting connected with others flows out of your complete connection to God. You must be connected to God to maximize your connection with others. Essentially, there is a standard operating procedure for getting and staying connected.

Sacrifice: In order to be in relationship with God, you must sacrifice your will for His. This is the ultimate in worship, bowing your will and taking on His so completely that you can't even remember what your will was. *What? I thought all I had to do was say, "God, I want You to be my Savior" and then He would accept me and things would be gravy from here on.* Yes, Jesus accepts you as you are, with your mistakes, failures, successes, pain, joy, laughter, tears. He accepts you as you are, but then He speaks a word over you. *"The thief cometh not, but for to steal, and to kill, and to destroy: but I am come that they might have life, and that they might have it more abundantly" (John 10:10).* Romans 10:10 says, *"For with the heart man believeth unto righteousness; and with the mouth confession is made unto salvation."*

God has a plan for your life, and until you acknowledge that He is the one with all the answers and submit to Him, you will not experience salvation. Until you make that sacrifice, you are not ready to be connected to God. You may not be ready to die and go to hell, but are you ready to be connected to Him?

Obedience: Doing what God says the way He says it. Two statements here: 1) delayed obedience is disobedience, and 2) disobedience brings curses. Obedience helps you to learn the ways of God. Obedience prepares you for the moment when that particular skill or attribute will be needed. God is not trying to control or manipulate you, but He knows what is coming up in your future and will prepare you to handle it if you will walk through today's lessons obediently.

Remember Mr. Miyagi and the Karate kid? *Daniel-san, wax on, wax off!* Daniel grumbled and complained but he did it. At the moment when those hard-won skills were most needed, he was able to pull them off. You see, training and equipping come before the action is needed. In every circumstance we must learn the pattern obedience teaches so that when the actual situation occurs we are equipped to handle it. Obedience to the commands of God is proof that you love Him.

Habits are formed by repetition. If you don't repeatedly do something it is not a habit. If you did it once you cannot consider it a habit. We need to be mindful of the habits we form. The habit of smoking is developed over time and the effects are great. The habit of obeying God is developed over time and the benefits are eternal. Develop the obedience habit.

Submission: Submission is more than obedience. Since we will cover this concept in depth in the following chapter, I'll keep it simple. Submission connects you to God because it demonstrates that you honor His authority. Submission is more of a heart attitude than outward operation. Outward obedience does not necessarily constitute an attitude of submission. It is possible to obey someone without ever submitting to his or her authority. It is important not to confuse the concepts of obedience and submission. When you learn the lesson of submission to God, you in turn will have a deeper understanding of the necessity of submission in your relationships. When you are submitted to God, you do not have a problems submitting to others. This builds your connection with people. This enhances your ability to develop a team and accomplish great things. When you realize God has made provision for you to accomplish the task by providing others to help you, it will change how you live.

God's View

God is a proponent of teams. He ordained it from the beginning with the creation of Adam and Eve. He worked, through teams in much of the Old Testament. He demonstrated it in the New Testament with the sending of the disciples. He even inspired Paul, to speak of the power of unity and connection in accomplishing the will of God through many of his epistles. Accomplishing the plan of God is a great work. It will take all of us to get it done. God equips each of us with unique gifts, skills, talents, preferences, and desires so that we can do our part to accomplish His plan. His desire is that we see the uniqueness of each other and allow them to come alongside us to complete the work. God gave us a marvelous example in the building of the tabernacle. Moses was given the plan and therefore was in charge, yet artisans had to come in and do their part in excellence to complete the work. Likewise, in our lives there is a plan. We must look out among those who are also called to do the same work and learn to connect with them that the work can move ahead with speed and power.

Achieving your purpose in life is much like the journey the children of Israel took out of Egypt going into the Promised Land. It is a journey out of bondage to sin into the freedom and liberty of God's love. On your journey, you are called to recognize that God is sovereign, and get rid of your old mindsets and behaviors and embrace the new. Doing everything by yourself is a part of the old man. God has declared it to be dead you must demonstrate that in your actions. God wants you to show that He is the provider of all that we need. Doing things all by yourself does not glorify God as much as seeing many of His children working to their full potential and in strong, healthy covenant relationships. If we fail to see that we need others to accomplish things we deny the original plan of God.

I am not saying that you cannot do things alone, God can and will equip you to do many things. You should trust Him and walk obediently as He directs you. What I am talking about is the mindset that shuts people out and does not accept what others have to offer because of an improper need to control things. This mindset ultimately comes out of fear. It hinders you and causes you to take on too much. It keeps you from being able to enjoy the things God has blessed with you as you are constantly working and struggling to stay ahead. God, our Father, desires that you have a real relationship with Him, that you work hard, but also that you enjoy the fruit of your labor. Being stressed out, frustrated and overwhelmed because of a lack of delegation or collaboration does not allow you to receive God's best for your life.

God didn't say do it all by yourself, so just as Jethro told Moses get some help, let me say to you: get some help. Maximize the power of the teamwork, do not try to do it all by yourself.

Renew Your Mind...

Think about the previous chapter. What challenged your thinking in this area? Take a moment and interact with the material by journaling your thoughts prior to reading and your thoughts now.

_____

_____

_____

_____

_____

_____

_____

_____

_____

Transform Your Walk...

Change occurs when we move from thinking to doing. Change involves action. What have you been doing all by yourself that you could allow someone to help you with? Make a list of those things and add the possible ways help could be infused into the situation.

_____

_____

_____

_____

_____

_____

_____

_____

_____

_____

Chapter Twelve

God Didn't Say...
Submission Is a Bad Word

*"Who, being in the form of God,
thought it not robbery to be equal with God:
But made himself of no reputation,
and took upon him the form of a servant, and was made
in the likeness of men: And being found in fashion
as a man, he humbled himself, and
became obedient unto death, even the death of the cross."
Philippians 2:6-8*

Setting the Stage

Submission has the ominous reputation of being a bad word, equally disdained in both the church and secular worlds. However, in the church, since submission is a requirement, we often understand it intellectually and want to obey but struggle with the practical application and experience of submitted life. We lack understanding of what it really means to submit.

In the church, the most common reference to submission is a strong admonition to wives. Repeatedly wives are told, "You must submit to your husband." Usually the context, whether intentional or unintentional, causes the wife to conjure up a picture of quietly giving in to everything her husband says. The woman feels as if she must be a spineless doormat to fulfill the mandate of the Lord. This is not the picture of submission God intended us to live by. Submission is not a lack of power, thought, or voice. It does not mean a person does not have backbone, right, or authority to say or do something. This faulty thinking stands in direct contradiction to God's view. An improper view of submission is the biggest contributor to rebellion against its practice. Submission is not a bad word, and therefore we cannot disregard it as a major component of a thriving Christian walk. Additionally, wives were not the only people told to submit in the Bible; husbands, servants, and workers, just to name a few.

In considering other facts that make submission challenging, it is important to face our own need to feel important. Our fear of being made unimportant keeps us from true submission.

Submission is comprised of two words, "sub" and "mission." This combination helps shed light on its true meaning. Sub means "under" and mission can be defined as a task or project. So in actuality submission has nothing to do with a lack of power; it has everything to do with unity and the fulfillment of purpose.

A submitted wife doesn't mean she is to be without a voice, opinion, or wisdom. It means she is committed to the fulfillment of mission of her husband or family. Our view of submission must be in line with God's view if we want to receive all that He has for us. We must reprogram our minds by accepting the true definition of the word *submission*. John 8:32 says, *"And ye shall know the truth, and the truth shall make you free."* When you experience the truth of submission, it will cause you to walk in liberty and power.

Addressing Spiritual Myths
Myth 1: If I have a thought, idea, or opinion about an issue I am not submitted to those in authority

By virtue of our training, and the popular portrayal of a "submitted" person, we believe that to speak up or offer a differing thought is to be unsubmitted or rebellious. This myth began and is perpetuated by those who want to be in complete control. In order to hold onto this belief, one must have a low opinion of themselves and their abilities. It is the dismantling of the human privilege of thinking. God gave each of us the ability to think. When we are continually told that our thoughts don't matter because someone else's way is the right way, simply because they are in charge, it erodes our ability to function as God intended. This myth gives way to a lowering of self-esteem and self-worth. When you hold this belief, either consciously or unconsciously, you begin to think you have nothing to offer in any situation. It saps your ability to make decisions and causes an increase in self-doubt. Doubt is an enemy to faith. After a period of time you start to believe it and live accordingly—afraid to speak up or speak out for fear of offending or being considered non-submissive or unsupportive. This myth is designed to silence you, shut you down. You must reject this thinking. You have value and worth to give to the earth.

Myth 2: To be submitted, I must always agree with the plan

Compliance gained by control is not the biblical standard of compliance. This myth is commonly perpetuated to control the actions of another. Since submission means "committed to the fulfillment of mission," we must recognize that people will be involved. The main issue with this myth is that it causes people to live with a sense of guilt. They feel guilty if they don't agree with the plan but are challenged to say something. A lack of agreement to a plan or strategy is not evidence of disunity but rather an opportunity to gain more information or to improve the plan. If the person in authority takes it personally, it is their issue. All you can do is reassure them that you support them and continue to move forward. If there is a lack of unity, each party involved should evaluate the situation and determine what the motivation and will of God is in the situation.

Myth 3: Outward obedience is evidence of submission

Outward obedience does not always translate to inward submission. It is possible to do the right thing outwardly and lack a real understanding of submission. Daily, people do what they have to do outwardly for a multitude of reasons, but their heart may be far from the mission. People have to work a certain way to keep a job, stay out of trouble, or even gain some kind of influence. Yet inwardly they do not believe in or care about the accomplishment of the mission. A lack of submission is a breeding ground for dishonor. Outward obedience coupled with inward submission is a powerful attribute.

Myth 4: I can be submitted to God but not man

The "I am submitted to God but not man" way of thinking is wrong. It is impossible to be submitted to God and not see the importance of submission in other relationships. If you are submitted to God, then you have accepted His authority. Keep in mind that submission is one of the highest demands placed on man. It is greater than works and deeds. Once you are submitted to God, all subsequent submission becomes easy.

Uncovering Spiritual Facts

To be submitted is to be completely committed to and supportive of the mission that must be accomplished. God has an implicit goal for every relationship we encounter. Marriage is to demonstrate Christ's love for the church.

Parenting demonstrates how we are to be submitted to one another in relationships of authority and instruction. When we are in a relationship, be it work, family, or school, there is a goal, purpose, or mission that God ordained to spring from its existence. In our relationships, we must get in alignment with that purpose. God made us all unique; He gave us all special gifts, talents, skills, and knowledge to help the mission get accomplished. When we think our opinions, thoughts, or ideas don't matter, we are embracing one of the myths about submission. The truth is that when we purposely withhold our thoughts, ideas, or even opinions we are not fully submitted to the project's success. To withhold information that might be vital to the life of the project or task is to be against its success. Remember the words of Jesus, "Whosoever is not for us is against us."

Actually, we can slay another mythological giant with this same stone. At times we may think that to demonstrate submission we must agree with the one who has responsibility or accountability for the mission. Yet a lack of agreement not driven by impure or self-serving motives only indicates that the best decision may not have been reached so far. It often proves move information is needed. God often puts flags, speed bumps, and other things in our way to slow us down so we can get divine wisdom to help make a wise choice. The Bible teaches that true wisdom comes from God and does not cause confusion or strife. *"But the wisdom that is from above is first pure, then peaceable, gentle, and easy to be entreated, full of mercy and good fruits, without partiality, and without hypocrisy" (James 3:17).* Sometimes disagreements will occur. In a time of disagreement, power, authority, and control should not be lorded over anyone, but the fruit of righteousness must prevail so that the best answer can be arrived at concerning the issue.

A special case in point would be leaders. It is important for those who have influence to remember that questions,

191

thoughts, and other ideas are not personal attacks against you. God desires that we all be valued, and often the opinions and thoughts of others are His reminder to leaders that we cannot do everything ourselves.

Conflict or disagreement doesn't have to be a bad word in the experience of a saint. Two don't become one flesh because of a loss of voice or personal identity. Two become one flesh as a result of divine submission. Submission causes us to separate our thoughts and desires and bring them in line with the Word of God. When people disagree, greater truth must be revealed in the situation. Of course there comes a time when a decision must be made and the one in authority has to make it. This place is where the "leader," the one deemed responsible, will have to make a final decision utilizing all the information they have. Having been given all the information and having heard discussion is the best place from which to make a righteous choice.

Imparting Truth About Submission

When you are a person whose inner makeup is composed of submission, it is evidenced in every facet of your life. It is impossible to be submitted to God but not to man. The key to submission is the realization that everyone is submitted to someone. There are no Lone Rangers in the kingdom of God.

The man or woman who is submitted unlocks the door to some powerful spiritual benefits. Although it seems paradoxical, proper submission brings great increase and protection into your life. Take the example of Mary and Joseph. Their submission to the Word and will of God was incredible. Their submission caused them to increase in wisdom, insight, and protection. The Holy Spirit told them when, where, and how to move. He protected them from danger by giving them insight on where to move. They were submitted to God and man. It would seem easy for them, having angelic visitations and being in the middle of the greatest miracle, to feel a sense of pride. As it was, God had spoken to them.

Everyone has to submit to someone. Yet above our personal submission to a person, we must recognize that our submission is really to the purpose and plan of God. Think about it: our submission to parents is really yielding to the plan of God for that relationship. Submission is not the same as obedience. We have erroneously thought the two are interchangeable. The reality of it is they each carry their own definition as well as application in our lives. Obedience and submission work together as a powerful team. Submission is to be placed in the proper arrangement congruent to the fulfillment of purpose.

The thoughts and opinions we have regarding submission are truly monumental.

God's View

Submission is the highest demand placed on man because it is tied to the foundational principle of the kingdom— the recognition of authority. Submission is not a bad word. It does mean to be a door mat or be void of thoughts, ideas, or opinions it means to accept authority and to come under it in order to accomplish a bigger mission. The one under authority must be aware of their position, have confidence in their ability, and be willing to support the one in authority for the sake of accomplishing the task. God places all things in proper order therefore we must recognize this and obey.

God is serious about submission. The biggest problem with submission is the lack of understanding how tied to authority it is. God desires that we submit to Him, as well as to our earthly leaders. A leader can be a parent, boss, pastor, etc.

At the heart of submission is the knowledge that God has a plan. Our trust and faith in that plan is the motivation to submit. God kicked Lucifer out of heaven because of a lack of submission. Lucifer had another plan. He didn't support the mission given and subsequently lost it all after staging a coup. He tried to assert his authority over God's. He lost his home, his job, his friends, and even his name.

A lack of submission is divisive. It creates a divide in the foundation of relationships. This division leads to a lack of success, for Jesus told us, "A house divided against itself cannot stand."

Submission is the key to mission accomplishment. God is not just concerned about "getting this done" but also about the manner in which things get done.

God didn't say submission is a bad word.

Renew Your Mind...

Think about the previous chapter. What challenged your thinking in this area? Take a moment and interact with the material by journaling your thoughts prior to reading and your thoughts now.

_____
_____
_____
_____
_____
_____
_____
_____
_____
_____

Transform Your Walk...

Change occurs when we move from thinking to doing. Change involves action. What were your views on submission prior to now? How can you practically apply this word to your life today?

_____
_____
_____
_____
_____
_____
_____
_____
_____
_____

Chapter Thirteen

God Didn't Say...
There Would Be No Conflict

*"Think not that I am come to send peace on earth:
I came not to send peace but a sword."*
Matthew 10:34

Setting the Stage

Jillian had a family problem. Her son was about to graduate from high school and wanted more freedom. In fact, he not only wanted it but he had already begun to live out his desires. He refused to adhere to established curfews. He often ignored requests to help out around the house. And he spoke to his mother disrespectfully. His behavior caused an internal and external conflict in Jillian. As a Christian woman devoted to applying the principles of her faith, the answer to the problem seemed clear: her son would simply have to abide by the rules of the house. Now enters the conflict. Her husband, also a committed Christian, looked at the situation differently. He decided it was best to give in to the demands of the son fearing that if they caused too much of a stir, it might alienate him. Interestingly enough, both Jillian and her husband were avoiding conflict—the husband with the son and Jillian with her husband. Jillian didn't agree that they should give in, but she didn't want to create a problem with her husband. Unsure of how to handle the problem, she sought the help of her Christian Life Coach. In one of her regular weekly sessions, she brought up the situation. Through some powerful questioning her coach helped her to understand a few things about the situation, and Jillian was able to align her thinking with her life.

The first discussions with her coach revealed some insightful information. She knew three things from many years of going to church: her husband was the head of the household, submission is required from a wife, and they were responsible for training their son. Although she knew these three things, she struggled with how to balance her knowledge with experience. These three issues moved around within her and caused even greater internal conflict because she could not figure out how to balance them all without upsetting someone. She was at a loss. It was clear that understanding conflict would be the key ingredient to overcoming this obstacle and improving their family situation. We addressed the need to remove fear of conflict from their lives. A conflict doesn't have to mean a lack of submission. It doesn't mean there is no love. It simply says we have two or more views that are not compatible. The best thing to do is to seek God's truth for how we are to behave in this instance and do it. It takes strength to recognize that conflict can sometimes be God's way of saying, "I'd like to have a say in this situation." For Jillian to avoid confrontation with her husband would not be biblical. It would undermine his ability to lead the family in a positive direction. With Jillian, we began to address the spiritual truths and myths at play in her situation.

Jillian's example is far too common. Somehow or another we have gotten to the place where we believe a good Christian life is void of conflict. For many people the prevailing thought is that conflict is a bad thing, something to be avoided in our lives. In fact, because of this belief many have become masterful avoiders of confrontation. Although few people enjoy conflict, avoiding it can have great spiritual implications. Avoiding conflict causes the lines between righteous and unrighteous living to be blurred. Evading conflict heightens our ability to ignore error. It causes us to disregard sin. We begin to ask ourselves questions like "Who said conflict is bad?" Who said in order to be a person of faith you have to avoid conflict? Conflict doesn't have to be avoided, but our focus should be on the guidelines God has given for resolving each situation. To move to a healthier spiritual understanding of conflict, we must be willing to address those things that cloud our vision.

Addressing Spiritual Myths
Myth 1: If I engage in conflict I might experience unbearable loss

The power of believing this myth is that it produces fear. The presence of fear is rooted in the fact that losing something would be the worst thing possible. It causes you to avoid conflict because of the thought that a relationship or situation cannot bear the stress of a disagreement. When our identity is tied to the things we possess, even relationships, we cannot bear the thought of losing them. The effects of this belief can come from a conscious or subconscious level of understanding. Regardless of whether it is conscious or subconscious, the existence of this thought causes a refusal to address situations appropriately. Sometimes the fear of losing a valued possession can be good if it translates into the proper protection, care, and keeping of that which is valued. However, when motivated by fear the boundaries and guidelines for care and protection are pushed beyond the normal limits. Whenever there is a fear of loss, people tend to hold on tightly to what they have. Believing this myth causes fear to grip your imagination and develop an entire roster of scenarios about loss.

Looking at Jillian's example, she was afraid to assert herself for fear that her husband might think she was against him. Matt, on the other had, was afraid he would alienate his son. Avoidance of conflict is based on the element of fear. This fear that he would lose his son kept him tied to the belief that he should not speak up or set a standard in his home. This way of thinking proved to be more destructive than constructive, as unwillingness to confront the situation spilled over into his marriage and began to take its toll there.

The fear of loss can be quite crippling in the execution of our lives. Sometimes we don't even know our thinking is being shaped from a position of fear. We simply tell ourselves that we are keeping the situation under control or even practicing the art of compromise. Fear is not of God. We know this intellectually, yet experientially our hearts get attached to something and our objectivity is skewed. God has given us the ability to overcome fear with power, love, and self-discipline. Fear of loss can be tied to a lack of trust in God or a failure to realize that God is the owner of everything. Matt was willing to diminish his role and responsibility as a parent to satisfy the desires of his son. Biblically, we also see this with Manoah and his wife, the parents of Samson. Their acquiescence to his whim caused him to end up losing his power, his anointing, and even his life.

Myth 2: Conflict should be avoided at all cost

There is no more tightly held belief about conflict than this one. Many people will do anything to avoid conflict. Techniques run the gamut of ignoring to going along with something just to keep the peace. We take on the attitude that we must grin and bear it if that is what it takes to avoid any conflict or confrontation. We have become masters at conflict avoidance, often allowing things to happen that are not in line with the will of God. Fortunately for us, God is able to cause all things to work together for our good (Romans 8:28). Samson's parents knew that God forbade mixed marriages, yet they wanted their son to be pleased. They didn't want the conflict that might ensue if they told him no so they said okay. Though you probably know the rest of the story, let's just recall that he lost his power and position because of conflict avoidance.

Be careful when your desire to avoid conflict causes you to diminish the word of the Lord. Although conflict doesn't have to be avoided at all cost, one should be careful not to be a conflict kamikaze either. We should not create conflict or jump into situations of conflict simply because we now have the liberty and knowledge to manage a situation.

Note: the prohibition of Israel and mixed marriage was not about color but religious culture. Israel was to honor the holiness of true worship and their relationship with God. God forbade it because of the potential for Israel to fall into idolatry. The children of Israel were to be pure from idolatry and serving other gods. Biblically, then this violated the standard of religious purity in that once one became involved with a person worshipping other gods; they could potentially begin to do the same thing. It was not an edict on race or social separation.

Myth 3: Conflict doesn't honor God

The enemy is so subtle he wants you to panic and believe that conflict dishonors God. *"Many are the afflictions of the righteous but the Lord shall deliver him from them all." (Psalm 34:19)* Conflict sets an atmosphere for God to be honored. How can two walk together unless they are agreed?

Honoring God is to esteem Him. When we accept this myth as fact, we demonstrate that we don't see a way to esteem God or bring glory to His name. Believing this myth is testimony to our lack of spiritual sight. Spiritual sight helps us to see situations and circumstances from a different point of view. Spiritual maturity causes you to see God in all situations. It doesn't take vision to see whether God isn't. It takes vision to see where He is. Likewise, it doesn't take a picture perfect situation to honor God; it takes a person willing to do what the Lord requires in that situation.

Get ready to be freed from this myth.

Uncovering Spiritual Truth

Truth 1: Your ability to engage in conflict cannot be controlled by fear

Fear of losing cannot dwell in the heart of a believer when it comes to skillfully engaging in conflict. Fear of losing something, whether it is a job, a possession, or even a relationship, should force us to examine where our dependency lies. If it is in God, then we trust Him to bring us through times of conflict in accordance with His will. If it is in the relationship itself, then we are bound to avoid conflict as we remain uncertain as to the stability of the relationship. Job lost everything, and God proved that despite any losses he suffered, restoration and compassion flow from heaven. We cannot put our trust in any man but in God alone.

Fear of loss is further associated with our inability to trust God. We are able to overcome this when we recognize and accept that God is the giver of everything. Job said, *"The Lord giveth and the Lord taketh away: blessed be the name of the Lord" (Job 1:21)*. Gain and loss come from the Lord's hand. God's plan is higher than ours. His working always tops ours. God sees the bigger picture. How much do we trust Him with the plan? We must overcome our limited thinking and our attempt to be masters of our universe. Loss is really never loss with God. His Word promises us that we are the head and not the tail, and that He will never leave us destitute. He will never leave us broken, cast down, or despised. God is our provision, and He knows what is best for us. When all is said and done, we must be willing to accept the will of the Lord without fear or complaint. Not only is our ability to engage in positive productive conflict at issue, but our continued spiritual growth and maturity.

Truth 2: Conflict cannot be avoided

The reality of living in a fallen world means that conflict will come. Not everyone is on the same page that has been written by the Holy Spirit. The word *conflict* itself is derived from the Greek word *agon,* meaning "a contest for victory or mastery, implying force or violence, strife, and intention." Conflict causes us to master a situation. If we avoid conflict, in essence we avoid the opportunity to master a situation in a godly manner. Conflict cannot be avoided.

To bury our heads in the sand further demonstrates our belief that there is no value in the will, way, or opinions of God. After all, when we engage in conflict we are to be led by the Spirit of God.

Truth 3: Belief in Jesus produces conflict

The words of Jesus Christ are so powerful to grasping this truth, for He said, "Think not that I am come to send peace on earth but a sword." If there was no honor to be realized through conflict, Jesus would never have made such a bold and radical statement. Christ teaches that conflict brings change. Change or transformation is the hallmark of Christianity. It must occur in us to reflect the glory of God. It must occur as meted out by us to bring the world into alignment with His will. If we are to accomplish the will of God on earth, we must demonstrate the same principles that are at work in heaven.

Not only does conflict bring change, but the reverse is equally true. Change brings conflict. When we have a prescribed method of doing things and that balance is upset, conflict arises. When conflict arises, we must find ways to resolve the conflict. It honors God to take His Word and apply it to a situation, thus proving the true power of His Word. God's Word is supernaturally effective. We don't have to hide behind the fear of dishonoring God to avoid confrontation.

If we fail to take advantage of opportunities to honor God, we fail to fully live up to our divine purpose.

The Value of Conflict

There is value and purpose to conflict in the lives of believers. We don't have to accept the world's methods for conflict management or resolution; rather we should embrace the Word of the Lord. Adherence to the Word brings the greatest, quickest, and cleanest resolution to any conflict we might have. How do we as believers resolve conflict? First, we must truly and as objectively as possible understand the situation. We must know what is at stake and what is being assaulted. Conflict is a spiritual warfare tactic. When we recognize what is really being assaulted, we are better equipped to handle the situation.

God's View

God does not cringe at the thought of conflict. In fact, conflict can be a powerful tool to help keep you out of the valley of indecisiveness, error, and compromise. Whenever there is conflict, there is a need for action. Each situation presents an opportunity for you to make a decision or demonstrate a behavior. Not just the decision that feels good to you or any action you feel like taking but an opportunity to manifest Gods' will. You can make a decision based on the Word of God. You can act in accordance with the Word of God. In the midst of conflict, you must decide to find a way to glorify God, and that is not found in the arena of conflict avoidance.

When faced with conflict, plug into God. Discern His will in the situation and allow the Holy Spirit to help you demonstrate more of His character and nature. God didn't say there would be no conflict; He simply wants an opportunity to be revealed in the situation.

Renew Your Mind...

What were your thoughts about conflict before reading this chapter? What are they now? Take a moment and interact with the material by journaling your thoughts prior to reading and your thoughts now.

_____
_____
_____
_____
_____
_____
_____
_____
_____
_____

Transform Your Walk...

Change involves action. True change occurs when we move from thinking to doing. What actions can you begin to take to demonstrate your new thoughts about conflict?

_____
_____
_____
_____
_____
_____
_____
_____
_____
_____

Conclusion

Don't Stop Here!

You are now at the crux of a life transforming decision. Are you ready to live a life of radical faith and real power? Can you handle moving into greater peace, power, and fulfillment? If your answer is, "Yes!" Then you should begin to put the word that you have learned into action immediately.

I am truly a believer that God wants us to live a life of radical faith. A life where we understand what we believe and consistently act in accordance with our belief. God has not called us to kamikaze type faith. His word provides evidence that brings you confidence and increases your trust. It is real. It produces power. Now, the ultimate in power has nothing to do with fame, fortune, or notoriety but it has everything to do with being able to maintain continuous fellowship with the Father and release His Spirit in your area of influence. You were created to have influence and you have been strategically placed where you are. A life that has real power is one that expands the kingdom wherever it is lived. Real power is the ability to reflect God's authority and dominion in the earth.

Having a clear understanding of the spiritual truth behind Gods word positions you for greater success. Whenever you understand what God really meant when he spoke, you have the power to raise your application of the Word in your life from legalistic to authentically practical. Understanding is the building block of experience, and experience is what you need to live a powerful, power-filled life. A powerful life is one that causes you to fulfill purpose and honor God in every area of your life. A power-filled life is one that has a positive impact and great influence on others. Both are essential to kingdom expansion. God wants you to have both. Let the principles uncovered here infuse you with the truth that will transform your life. Take some time to put them into practice in your life. You must continually press to move beyond the surface. Recognize the spiritual reality behind every statement God makes. Your understanding and application is the key to revealing your identity and giving you power. James 1:22-25 says, *"But be ye does of the word, and not hearers only, deceiving your own selves. For if any be a hearer of the word, and not a doer, he is like unto a man beholding his natural face in a glass; for he beholdeth himself, and goeth his way, and straightway forgetteth what manner of man he was But whoso looketh into the perfect law of liberty, and continueth therein, he being not a forgetful hearer, but a doer of the work, this man shall be blessed in his deed."*

God designed your life to prove His will. His will is good, perfect, and acceptable. Employing the spiritual truths revealed in *God Didn't Say That* will indeed move from intellectual Christianity to powerful faith-filled living.

"You have heard that it was said by them of old time, "thou shalt.... But I say unto you." Those words still echo within me as a powerful reminder of the importance of knowing the spirit of the law not just the letter. I pray that the previous pages have given you insight to the spiritual meaning of the Word of the Lord as well as practical application. As you stand now, you can declare, gone are the days when you settled for knowing the letter of the law.

Remember the words of Paul, *"...for the letter killeth, but the spirit giveth life."* 2 Corinthians 3:6

Experiencing the power of the Word of God comes only as you answer the call to deeper understanding, followed by a big step of obedient application. May you answer the call and take that step today!

Blessings to you!

God Didn't Say That
Quick Reference Chart

God Didn't Say...	Scriptural Thought	You Really Need To Know This
Apologize	*"If we confess our sins, He is faithful and righteous to forgive us our sins and to cleanse us from all unrighteousness."* I John 1:9	Apology is not the same as confession
There Would Be No Consequences	*"Before I was afflicted I went astray: but now have I kept thy word."* Psalm 119:67	Consequences are not to be avoided
Obedience is Optional	*"And Samuel said, Hath the Lord as great delight in burnt offerings and sacrifices, as in obeying the voice of the Lord? Behold, to obey is better than sacrifice, and to hearken than the fat of rams."* I Samuel 15:22	Obedience is an act of worship

God Didn't Say...	Scriptural Thought	You Really Need To Know This
Performance Equals Purpose	*"Not every one that saith unto me, Lord, Lord, shall enter into the kingdom of heaven; but he that doeth the will of my Father which is in heaven."* Matthew 7:21	Your relationship with God matters more than performance
Ask for anything you want	*"Delight thyself also in the Lord; and he shall give thee the desires of thine heart."* Psalm 37:4	God answers prayer according to His plan
There Would Never Be Pain	*"For our light affliction, which is but for a moment, worketh for us a far more exceeding and eternal weight of glory."* 2 Corinthians 4:17	Pain proceeds the revelation of glory
Love is Negotiable	*"A new commandment I give unto you, That ye love one another; ad I have loved you, that ye also love one another. By this shall all men know that ye are my disciples, if ye have love one to another"* John 13:34-35	Love is the essential mark of a Christian

God Didn't Say...	Scriptural Thought	You Really Need To Know This
Things Will Never Change	*"And the manna ceased on the morrow after they had eaten of the old corn of the land; neither had the children of Israel manna any more; but they did eat of the fruit of the land of Canaan that year."* Joshua 5:12	God may change His methods but His principles remain the same.
Forgive If You Feel Like It	*"But if ye forgive not men their trespasses, neither will your Father forgive your trespasses."* Matthew 6:15	Forgiveness releases power
Trust Is the Same As Belief	*"Commit thy way unto the Lord: trust also in him; and he shall bring it to pass."* Psalm 37:5	There is a powerful belief-trust connection

God Didn't Say...	Scriptural Thought	You Really Need To Know This
Do It All By Yourself	*"And he gave some apostles; and some, prophets; and some evangelists; and some, pastors and teachers; for the perfecting of the saints, for the work of the ministry, for the edifying of the body of Christ: till we all come in the unity of the faith, and of the knowledge of the Son of God, unto a perfect man, unto the measure of the stature of the fullness of Christ." Ephesians 4:11-12*	Strong support systems increase your effectiveness

God Didn't Say...	Scriptural Thought	You Really Need To Know This
Submission Is a Bad Word	*"Who, being in the form of God, thought it not robbery to be equal with God: But made himself of no reputation, and took upon him the form of a servant, and was made in the likeness of men: And being found in fashion as a man, he humbled himself, and became obedient unto death, even the death of the cross." Philippians 2:6-8*	Honor authority in your life
There Would Be No Conflict	*"Think not that I am come to send peace on earth: I came not to send peace but a sword." Matthew 10:34*	Manage conflict skillfully

To Contact Mikaela Cade

For speaking engagements, please email your requests to:
requests@mikaelacade.com

For other inquiries, please send your email requests to:
info@mikaelacade.com

To learn more about connecting with MCM visit us at:

www.mikaelacade.com

You can also write:

Mikaela Cade Ministries
P.O. BOX 936
Acworth, GA 30101
or call: (800) 874-4309
Email: info@mikaelacade.com